W9-CGM-533

ICEBOX DESSERTS

Also by Lauren Chattman

Icebox Pies

Mom's Big Book of Baking

Instant Gratification

Just Add Water

Cool Kitchen

100 COOL RECIPES FOR
ICEBOX CAKES, PIES,
PARFAITS, MOUSSES,
PUDDINGS, AND MORE

ICEBOX DESSERTS

LAUREN CHATTMAN

Photography by Duane Winfield

The Harvard Common Press
Boston, Massachusetts

The Harvard Common Press
535 Albany Street
Boston, Massachusetts 02118
www.harvardcommonpress.com

Copyright © 2005 by Lauren Chattman
Photographs copyright © 2005 by Duane Winfield

All rights reserved. No part of this publication may be reproduced or transmitted in any form or by any means, electronic or mechanical, including photocopying, recording, or any information storage or retrieval system, without permission in writing from the publisher.

Printed in China

Library of Congress Cataloging-in-Publication Data
Chattman, Lauren.
   Icebox desserts : 100 cool recipes for icebox cakes, pies, parfaits, mousses, puddings,
   and more / Lauren Chattman.
      p. cm.
      Includes index.
   ISBN 1-55832-270-1 (hc : alk. paper) -- ISBN 1-55832-271-X (pb : alk. paper)
     1. Desserts. 2. Frozen desserts. I. Title.
  TX773.C472 2005
  641.8′6--dc22

                                                  2004021151

Special bulk-order discounts are available on this and other Harvard Common Press books. Companies and organizations may purchase books for premiums or resale, or may arrange a custom edition, by contacting the Marketing Director at the address above.

10 9 8 7 6 5 4 3 2

Interior and cover design by Night & Day Design
Photography by Duane Winfield
Food styling by Megan Fawn Schlow and Mariann Sauvion
Prop styling by Duane Winfield and Justin Schwartz
Art direction by Justin Schwartz
Props included on pages 7, 98-99, and 119 were generously provided by
Le Creuset of America, Inc. (www.lecreuset.com)

For my family

Acknowledgments

Once again, I am grateful to Pam Hoenig for bringing this idea to me and for helping to transform it into a book. Heartfelt thanks to my new editor, Valerie Cimino, for her enthusiasm and sensitive handling of the manuscript in its final stage. Thanks to Bruce Shaw, Christine Alaimo, Betsy Young, Skye Stewart, Liza Beth, Sunshine Erickson, Abbey Phalen, Virginia Downes, Christine Corcoran Cox, Jodi Marchowsky, and Pat Jalbert-Levine for all of their support and hard work. Copyeditor Karen Levy made sure everything was just right. I'm so grateful to Suzanne Heiser for her fresh and attractive cover and book design. And I was so happy when I found out that Duane Winfield would be taking the photos for this book. They perfectly express the fun that I had developing these recipes. Thanks to Justin Schwartz for his art direction and Megan Fawn Schlow and Mariann Sauvion for their food styling. As always, Angela Miller was always around for excellent advice and entertaining conversation. And thanks to Jack, Rose, and Eve for gathering around the refrigerator and asking, "What's for dessert tonight?"

CONTENTS

BEYOND ICEBOX PIES

A couple of years ago I was given the terrific opportunity to write a book about icebox pies. I defined "icebox pie" as a simple dessert with a cookie crumb crust and a no-bake filling. Just the way a pumpkin pie had to bake in the oven before it was ready to eat, an icebox pie had to sit in the refrigerator or freezer to set up properly. Not only did "icebox" refer to the homey, nostalgic style of these desserts, but it also named the appliance essential for making them.

It was a joy and a challenge to come up with almost 100 different ways to fill an icebox pie. I whipped up icebox pudding pies, icebox mousse pies, and ice cream pies of every flavor. But once in a while I would come up with an idea for something yummy from the icebox that just didn't fit into a pie shell, and that was frustrating. Certainly my recipe for Beautiful Strawberry and Cream Trifle (see page 73) would be of interest to anyone who enjoyed desserts

from the refrigerator, and yet there was no way I could transform those layers of pastry cream, berries, and pound cake into a pie. Likewise, my idea for alternating pistachio ice cream, kirsch, and cherries in sundae dishes, then freezing it until dinnertime, although certainly "icebox" material, was not destined to be material for *Icebox Pies*.

As my friends and family well know, I am as frugal with my recipe ideas as I am with broken ice cream cones (which I save in a zipper-top bag in my freezer until I have enough to make a piecrust). I filed away the icebox ideas not destined for pie-dom, and kept going. And then, after *Icebox Pies* was published, I had my chance to review the subject from a wider angle. Pam Hoenig, my editor at The Harvard Common Press and the source of the idea for *Icebox Pies*, asked me whether I'd like to do a book on icebox desserts. Well, of course I said yes! I had already begun to write that book in my head.

And here it is, a collection of scrumptious desserts for every taste and every occasion. As the term "icebox" suggests, many of the recipes have an old-fashioned flavor. They are all beautiful and special, but with a homemade look rather than a professional gloss. "Icebox" should also suggest the ease with which they can be made and served. Today, we take for granted the amazing workhorse capabilities of our refrigerators and freezers, but back when the term icebox was coined, the refrigerator was absolutely worshiped for its ability to chill food and keep it fresh. I hope that these recipes will return you to that not-so-distant time when real home cooking was suddenly made simpler with the exciting arrival of the icebox.

When I began *Icebox Pies*, I barely knew what one was, let alone what kinds I wanted to include in my book. I had to formulate a definition before I could go into the kitchen. I decided that a true icebox pie was not just any old pie that had spent some time in the refrigerator. It had to have a simple crumb crust that needed only a few minutes in the oven to crisp up; rolling and baking pastry dough was too time-consuming and difficult for a book of simple desserts. Its filling would have to be uncooked or cooked on the stovetop; none of these pies would be baked and none would have meringue or brûlée toppings that would have to be broiled. And it would have to be well chilled before serving; every pie would set up in the refrigerator or freezer rather than in the oven.

So when I got to work on *Icebox Desserts* I already had an idea of what kinds of desserts would qualify. For me, a true icebox dessert requires no baking. Many simply involve mixing together or layering the ingredients, with no cooking at all. Any cooking happens on top of the stove. Once an icebox dessert is put together (a lot of them are more like little construction projects than recipes), it absolutely must spend time in either the refrigerator or the freezer before it can be considered ready to eat.

Now that I didn't have that pesky piecrust requirement, I was able to concentrate on coming up with icebox desserts of every shape and size: the simplest stovetop puddings (don't underestimate their scrumptiousness, though!); mousses, the lighter, airier relatives of puddings; parfaits of all sorts; what I call "icebox spectaculars"—trifles and charlottes—which are truly grand desserts but easy to make; icebox cakes and pies; gelatin-based desserts (no, not Jell-O, but rather its uptown cousin); all sorts of fun and sometimes eye-popping desserts made with store-bought ice creams and sorbets; and, finally, icebox cookies and confections, including new versions of the first icebox dessert I ever made—Marshmallow Fluff fudge.

Icebox Ingredients

The recipes in this book were designed with ease in mind. This means easy shopping, too—almost every ingredient may be found at your local supermarket. Just as ingredient lists for baked goods rely on a short list of staples—flour, sugar, baking powder—so do those for icebox desserts, but the list looks a little different. Here it is, along with shopping and handling details:

Chocolate: I use chocolate in every category of icebox desserts, so I've had a lot of opportunities to experiment. Premium brands such as Lindt, Ghirardelli, and Callebaut deliver smooth texture and rich flavor. Inexpensive baking chocolate should be reserved for baking. It is too grainy and sweet for icebox desserts.

Cookies and cookie crumbs: Graham crackers, Oreos, vanilla wafers, ladyfingers, gingersnaps—the cookie aisle of the supermarket is probably the most important place for gathering icebox dessert ingredients.

Cornstarch: This is an easy-to-use thickener for puddings. To prevent lumps from forming, be sure to dissolve cornstarch in water and whisk before adding it.

Eggs: Eggs thicken as well as enrich a variety of icebox desserts. All the recipes in this book were tested with large eggs. Usually, I heat eggs to a safe temperature of 160°F when preparing egg-based fillings, but there are a couple of recipes included that call for raw eggs. Because of the remote but dangerous possibility that raw eggs carry salmonella, they should not be used in food to be consumed by children, pregnant women, elderly people, or anyone in poor health or with a compromised immune system.

Fruit: Fresh fruit in season is key if a recipe calls for uncooked fruit. If fruit is to be cooked on top of the stove, I will occasionally buy individually quick frozen (IQF) fruit when fresh isn't available. Whether or not frozen fruit may be substituted for fresh is noted in individual recipes.

Gelatin: A flavorless, colorless thickener, gelatin comes in individual packets of powder and must be dissolved in cold water, then melted over hot water (if it's not going to be added to a hot mixture) before being used to turn a liquid into a solid.

Heavy cream: There wouldn't be many icebox desserts without heavy cream. See page 34 for tips on whipping it to its greatest volume.

Ice cream, sherbet, and sorbet: I prefer premium brands such as Häagen-Dazs and Ben & Jerry's when it comes to ice cream. The high butterfat content of these ice creams makes for richer, better-tasting desserts. As for sherbet and sorbet, I have to admit I am mostly guided by looks. For my Rainbow Sorbet Bombe (page 141) I just buy the most vividly colored sherbets in the freezer case.

Liqueurs, wines, and spirits: Grand Marnier, kirsch, framboise, bourbon, champagne, Scotch—I use small quantities of these to add depth and flavor to icebox desserts. Tiny bottles of liqueurs and spirits are economical and convenient when you don't want to invest in a large bottle of a liqueur you won't be drinking any time soon.

Pound cake: The trifle and cake recipes in this book were tested with Sara Lee all-butter frozen pound cake. Use it straight from the freezer. It will defrost quickly once sliced.

Icebox Equipment

In addition to your refrigerator and freezer, you will need some other basic kitchen equipment to create the desserts in this book. If you cook at all, you probably have most of the items listed below. The rest can be picked up at housewares shops and discount stores as you need them. (I've learned the hard way to scan a recipe enough in advance to run out and buy or borrow that missing loaf pan.)

Aluminum foil, plastic wrap, parchment, and waxed paper: Buy a roll of each of these and you will be able to wrap your desserts properly to keep them from sticking to the containers in which you are storing them, and to keep them fresh.

Baking pans: A few standard sizes will allow you to make all kinds of desserts. For fudge and cookies, an 8-inch square pan is necessary. You will need a 9½ x 4 x 3-inch loaf pan to make some of the ice cream and mousse ter-rines. (If you ever want to bake a from-scratch pound cake, you can use this same pan.) A 10-inch round cake pan will mold a Chocolate and Orange Icebox Bavarian Cake (see page 88). A 9-inch springform pan is used for cheesecakes.

Baking sheets: These come in handy for assembling some of the desserts. Rimmed sheets are best to catch drips and crumbs.

Electric mixer: I use a heavy-duty KitchenAid mixer, but a hand-held mixer will work just fine for whipping cream, beating cream cheese, and accomplishing other icebox tasks.

Food processor: This is a great tool for chopping nuts, turning cookies into crumbs, and pureeing fruit.

Measuring cups and spoons: For best results with these recipes, measure accurately and carefully with glass or clear plastic "liquid" measuring cups for liquid ingredients and plastic or metal "dry" measuring cups for large quantities of dry ingredients. For small quantities, use measuring spoons. Fill cups and spoons completely and level off dry ingredients with a knife for accurate measurements.

Parfait glasses: There's a whole chapter of parfait recipes, and if you want to make any of them you will need something to put them in. But don't make a big investment if you don't possess special parfait glasses. Chances are you have some type of glassware that can be substituted: martini glasses, margarita glasses, sundae dishes, little compotes, and even old-fashioned glasses and highballs can look great and work well, depending on the recipe.

Pie pan: The recipes in this book call for a 9-inch pie pan. I prefer glass pans because of their even baking, but if you already have a metal pan, it will work fine.

Ramekins: Individual porcelain ramekins are used to make panna cottas and other single-serving icebox desserts. When a particular size is needed, it is specified in the recipe.

Ring mold: A 1-quart ring mold is nice to have on hand for making frozen mousses and large gelatin desserts. Substitute a 1-quart bowl if you don't have a mold. It won't make as pretty a dessert, but it will do the job.

Saucepan: Any cooking of icebox desserts takes place on top of the stove, so a saucepan will be necessary from time to time. If you are in the market for a new one, spend a little extra money for a heavy anodized aluminum or stainless steel pan from a quality maker such as All-Clad or Calphalon. The extra weight will prevent your puddings and custards from scorching.

Spatulas: Flexible rubber spatulas are helpful for scrap-ing fillings from bowls and folding whipped cream together with other ingredients. Offset metal spatulas (both small and large) are good for smoothing fillings and frosting cakes and pies.

Strainer: A fine mesh strainer is essential for removing any lumps from puddings and custards. It is also handy for removing seeds and strings from fruit purees.

Tart pan: For the tarts in this book, you will need a 10-inch tart pan with a removable bottom. Four-inch tartlet pans are also nice for creating individual-serving tarts.

Trifle dish: This is a large, footed glass dish that displays layered desserts beautifully. A large glass bowl may be used in its place.

Wire whisks: A whisk will break up a lump that a spoon or spatula might miss. It's a very important item in the icebox dessert kitchen if you want smooth, not lumpy, desserts.

CHAPTER 1

Simply Perfect Puddings

Pudding satisfies the primal need for something sweet, smooth, and easy. There's nothing challenging about pudding. It aims to please, not provoke. That's not to say that pudding must be boring. The desserts in this chapter are designed to comfort you just the way your favorite childhood puddings did. But I hope they will also open your eyes to the range of interesting and even exotic desserts that can still call themselves puddings.

The terrific thing about pudding is that it is as easy to make as it is to eat. Each recipe in this chapter is basically cooked in one pot on top of the stove. But don't get too cocky. It is possible to make a bad pudding—one with lumps or the texture of rubbery Jell-O. Take care to follow the tips in the headnotes and recipe directions for the smoothest, silkiest, most perfect puddings.

Vanilla Custard Sauce with Fruit *Serves 6*

Don't underestimate this old-fashioned dessert, a custard sauce that enhances almost any fruit, from sliced strawberries in the early summer to fresh figs later on to poached pears in the middle of winter. The technique is simple but must be observed carefully. Cook the custard very slowly over low heat, stirring constantly. Remove it from the heat as soon as it begins to thicken and don't let it come to a boil, or you'll risk curdling the eggs (which is what I did the first time I tried it).

2 cups half-and-half
5 large egg yolks
⅔ cup sugar
⅛ teaspoon salt
1 teaspoon vanilla extract
4 cups fresh fruit cut into bite-size pieces
Sweetened whipped cream (optional)

1. Heat the half-and-half in a small heavy saucepan over medium heat until almost boiling. Remove from the heat.

2. Whisk the egg yolks, sugar, and salt together vigorously in a medium-size heavy saucepan until light in color, 2 to 3 minutes. Slowly drizzle in the hot half-and-half, whisking constantly. Cook over low heat, stirring constantly with a wooden spoon, until it just starts to thicken and bubble around the edges, 12 to 15 minutes. Do not let boil.

3. Remove from the heat and pour the mixture through a fine mesh strainer into a heatproof bowl. Don't scrape the bottom of the pot; that's where any lumps and burnt bits might be hiding. Stir in the vanilla. Set the bowl in a larger bowl of ice and water and let stand, whisking occasionally, until cool and thickened. Cover with plastic wrap and refrigerate until well chilled, at least 3 hours and up to 3 days.

4. To serve, spoon the custard into shallow dessert bowls and top with the fruit and a small dollop of whipped cream, if desired.

Milk Chocolate Custard Sauce with Pound Cake *Serves 8*

This chocolate custard is wonderful served as embellishment for either chocolate or vanilla pound cake, with a scattering of fresh berries. Homemade cake is great, but the beauty of this recipe is that it dresses up store-bought cake so you don't have to take the time to bake your own, if you don't want to. Bittersweet or semisweet chocolate may be substituted if you prefer.

7 ounces milk chocolate

2 tablespoons unsalted butter

2 cups half-and-half

5 large egg yolks

⅓ cup sugar

⅛ teaspoon salt

1 teaspoon vanilla extract

One 10- to 12-ounce store-bought pound cake or homemade from your favorite recipe

1 pint fresh raspberries, blackberries, or hulled and sliced strawberries

1. Bring 2 inches of water in a medium-size saucepan to a bare simmer. Place the chocolate and butter in a stainless-steel bowl big enough to rest on top of the saucepan and set it over the pan, making sure it doesn't touch the water. Heat, whisking occasionally, until completely melted. Remove from the heat and whisk until smooth. Set aside to cool.

2. Heat the half-and-half in a small heavy saucepan over medium heat until almost boiling. Remove from the heat.

3. Whisk together the egg yolks, sugar, and salt in a medium-size heavy saucepan, then whisk in the chocolate. Slowly drizzle in the hot half-and-half, whisking constantly. Cook over medium-low heat, stirring constantly with a wooden spoon, until it just starts to thicken and bubble around the edges, 12 to 15 minutes. Do not let boil.

4. Remove from the heat and pour through a fine mesh strainer into a heatproof bowl. Don't scrape the bottom of the pot; that's where any lumps and burnt bits might be hiding. Stir in the vanilla. Cover with plastic wrap and refrigerate until chilled and thickened, at least 3 hours and up to 3 days. Whisk before using.

5. To serve, pour some of the sauce on each of 8 dessert plates. Place a slice of pound cake on top of the sauce, then scatter the berries around the cake.

Spiked Butterscotch Pudding *Serves 4*

A little Scotch whiskey adds an indescribably delicious layer of flavor to this rich but simple pudding. This makes a very respectable casual dinner party dessert when served in parfait glasses and topped with whipped cream. Other liquors may be substituted to taste—rum and bourbon are both very good; for a kid-friendly version, more suitable for weeknights and after-school snacking, substitute one teaspoon of vanilla extract.

3 tablespoons unsalted butter
½ cup plus 2 tablespoons firmly packed dark brown sugar
⅛ teaspoon salt
3 tablespoons cornstarch
2 cups half-and-half
1½ tablespoons Scotch whiskey
Whipped cream (optional)

1. Combine the butter, brown sugar, and salt in a medium-size heavy saucepan and cook over low heat, whisking, until the butter is melted and the sugar has dissolved.

2. Whisk together the cornstarch and ½ cup of the half-and-half in a measuring cup until the cornstarch dissolves. Set aside.

3. Add ½ cup of the half-and-half to the saucepan and whisk until combined. Add the remaining 1 cup of half-and-half and the cornstarch mixture and stir to combine. Increase the heat to medium-high and cook, whisking, until thickened, 3 to 4 minutes. Remove from the heat and stir in the whiskey.

4. Spoon the pudding into 4 ramekins or dessert goblets but don't scrape the bottom of the pot; that's where any lumps and burnt bits might be hiding. Cover the surface of each pudding with a piece of plastic wrap to prevent a skin from forming. Refrigerate until chilled, at least 3 hours and up to 1 day.

5. Spoon some whipped cream on top of each portion, if desired, just before serving.

Chocolate Pudding for Beginners *Serves 4*

This is so simple to make that even those of you who are only vaguely familiar with that area of the home called the kitchen will be able to concoct a perfect batch the first time around. After experiencing such success, you will wonder why people buy instant pudding mix, when homemade is such child's play.

¼ cup cornstarch

6 tablespoons sugar

½ cup whole milk

2 cups half-and-half

6 ounces bittersweet chocolate, finely chopped

1 tablespoon unsalted butter

1 teaspoon vanilla extract

1. Combine the cornstarch and sugar in a medium-size heavy saucepan. Whisk in the milk until smooth. Add the half-and-half and bring to a boil, whisking constantly. Cook over medium-high heat, whisking, until thickened, 3 to 4 minutes.

2. Remove from the heat and add the chocolate, butter, and vanilla. Whisk until the chocolate and butter have melted and the pudding is very smooth.

3. Spoon into 4 dessert goblets or ramekins but don't scrape the bottom of the pot; that's where any lumps and burnt bits might be hiding. Cover the surface of each pudding with a piece of plastic wrap to prevent a skin from forming. Refrigerate until chilled, at least 1 hour and up to 1 day.

Superb Chocolate Pudding *Serves 4*

Once you have mastered chocolate pudding thickened with cornstarch, you might want to raise the stakes and attempt a more complex version. Here is my absolute favorite, made with bittersweet and unsweetened chocolate and a little bit of cocoa powder and enriched with a couple of egg yolks.

2 large egg yolks

½ cup plus 2 tablespoons sugar

2 tablespoons cornstarch

¼ cup unsweetened cocoa powder

2 cups half-and-half

2 ounces bittersweet chocolate, finely chopped

1½ ounces unsweetened chocolate, finely chopped

1 tablespoon unsalted butter

1 teaspoon vanilla extract

1. In a medium-size bowl, using an electric mixer, beat together the egg yolks and ½ cup of the sugar until thick and pale, about 4 minutes.

2. Combine the cornstarch, the remaining 2 tablespoons of sugar, and the cocoa in a medium-size heavy saucepan. Add ½ cup of the half-and-half and whisk until smooth. Whisk in the remaining 1½ cups of half-and-half and bring to a boil over medium heat, whisking constantly. Quickly whisk about one-third of the half-and-half mixture into the egg and sugar mixture, then whisk the egg mixture into the saucepan. Continue to whisk over medium heat until the mixture comes to a simmer, then let simmer, whisking constantly, for 1 minute.

3. Remove from the heat and whisk in both chocolates and the butter. Whisk until melted and the pudding is smooth. Stir in the vanilla.

4. Pour the pudding into 4 dessert goblets or ramekins, but don't scrape the bottom of the pot; that's where lumps are. Cover the surface of each pudding with plastic wrap to prevent a skin from forming. Refrigerate until chilled, at least 1 hour and up to 1 day.

Superb Chocolate Pudding, Five Different Ways

I like to vary this pudding, depending on my mood or what I have in the pantry. Here are some of my favorite variations:

- **Mexican Chocolate Pudding**: Whisk in ½ teaspoon of ground cinnamon with the cocoa.
- **Spicy Chocolate Pudding:** Whisk in ⅛ teaspoon of cayenne pepper with the cocoa.
- **Espresso-Chocolate Pudding:** Whisk in 1 tablespoon of instant espresso powder with the cocoa.
- **Chocolate-Mint Pudding**: Stir in ¼ teaspoon of peppermint extract with the vanilla.
- **Amaretto Chocolate Pudding**: Stir in 2 tablespoons of amaretto or other almond liqueur with the vanilla.

Honey-Almond Semolina Pudding *Serves 6*

Until I began to research pudding, I had no idea that my favorite hot cereal from childhood could be used to make a wonderful dessert. Apparently, Mediterranean cooks have been using semolina in pudding for hundreds of years. I use regular (as opposed to quick-cooking or instant) Cream of Wheat. It takes a few minutes longer, but the result is a creamier pudding.

⅓ cup sliced almonds
3 cups whole milk
½ cup honey
½ cup Cream of Wheat cereal
2 large egg yolks
⅓ cup sweetened dried cranberries
1 teaspoon almond extract
¾ cup heavy cream

1. Preheat the oven to 350°F. Spread the almonds on a baking sheet and toast until golden, 7 to 10 minutes. Watch carefully because soon after they become golden, they will begin to burn. Set aside to cool.

2. Bring the milk and 6 tablespoons of the honey to a boil in a medium-size heavy saucepan, whisking occasionally. Reduce the heat to low, whisk in the Cream of Wheat, and cook, stirring constantly, until thickened, about 10 minutes.

3. Remove from the heat and quickly whisk in the egg yolks, cranberries, and almond extract. Pour into a heatproof bowl and let cool just to room temperature, stirring occasionally so lumps don't form.

4. Combine the cream and remaining 2 tablespoons of honey in a medium-size bowl and beat, using an electric mixer, until stiff peaks form. Fold into the cooled Cream of Wheat mixture, being careful not to deflate the cream. Spoon into 6 dessert goblets and chill until ready to serve, at least 1 hour and up to 6 hours.

5. Just before serving, sprinkle each portion with some of the toasted almonds.

Cinnamon-Raisin Rice Pudding *Serves 6*

This is diner-style pudding, but it's not at all rubbery or chalky-tasting, like most truck stop versions. Egg yolks make it rich like custard and give it a creaminess that milk alone doesn't. I like golden raisins, but dark raisins are good, too, or you could leave them out entirely if you don't like raisins in your rice pudding. Parboiling the rice in water before cooking it in milk ensures that your rice will soften properly in a reasonable amount of time. After many attempts to eliminate this step, each one resulting in unpleasantly crunchy pudding, I take this precaution with every type of rice pudding I make.

Pinch of salt
½ cup long-grain rice
3 cups whole milk
1 cinnamon stick, broken in half
¾ cup sugar
2 large eggs
2 large egg yolks
½ cup heavy cream
½ cup golden raisins
1 teaspoon vanilla extract

1. Bring a large saucepan of water to a boil. Add the salt and rice, return to a boil, and continue to boil until the rice is almost tender, about 15 minutes. Drain well.

2. Combine the boiled rice, milk, cinnamon stick, and sugar in the same saucepan (no need to wash it; just empty the water). Bring to a boil, reduce the heat to low, and simmer, uncovered, stirring frequently, until the rice is very tender and the mixture somewhat reduced but still soupy, 20 to 25 minutes.

3. Whisk together the whole eggs and egg yolks in a medium-size bowl. In a small saucepan, bring the cream to a bare simmer, then drizzle into the eggs, whisking constantly. Whisk the egg-and-cream mixture into the rice. Simmer, stirring frequently, until the pudding just begins to thicken, about 1 minute. Remove from the heat and stir in the raisins and vanilla.

4. Spoon into 6 dessert goblets or ramekins. Cover the surface of each pudding with a piece of plastic wrap to prevent a skin from forming. Refrigerate until chilled, at least 3 hours and up to 2 days.

Couscous and Orange-Caramel Pudding *Serves 6*

Couscous enriched with egg yolks is a quick alternative to rice pudding. To transform this humble pudding into a dinner party dessert, I pour it into little ramekins and garnish with caramel sauce.

Orange-Caramel Sauce

¾ cup sugar

¼ cup water

½ cup heavy cream

3 tablespoons Grand Marnier or other orange liqueur

Pudding

3 cups whole milk

⅓ cup sugar

⅛ teaspoon salt

1 cup couscous

2 egg yolks

1 teaspoon vanilla extract

½ teaspoon grated orange zest

¼ cup shelled unsalted pistachios, chopped

1. To make the caramel sauce, bring the sugar and water to a boil in a small heavy saucepan and continue to boil until it turns a light amber color. Do not stir. If part of the syrup is turning darker than the rest, gently tilt the pan to even out the cooking. When the syrup is a uniform amber color, stir in the heavy cream with a long-handled spoon. Be careful, because it will bubble up. Transfer to a heatproof measuring cup and stir in the Grand Marnier. Let cool, then transfer to an airtight container. It will keep at room temperature for up to 1 week.

2. To make the pudding, bring 1½ cups of the milk, the sugar, and the salt to a boil in a medium-size heavy saucepan. Stir in the couscous, cover, remove from the heat, and let stand until the milk has been absorbed and the couscous is tender, about 10 minutes. Fluff with a fork to separate the grains.

3. Meanwhile, whisk together the egg yolks, vanilla, and orange zest in a medium-size bowl. In a small heavy saucepan over medium heat, heat the remaining 1½ cups of milk until just bubbling around the edges. Slowly drizzle into the egg yolks, whisking constantly. Whisk the egg yolk mixture into the couscous pot. Turn the heat to medium-high and cook, stirring constantly, until the pudding just starts to thicken, about 2 minutes.

4. Generously butter six 6-ounce ramekins and divide the pudding among them. Cover with plastic wrap and refrigerate until chilled, at least 3 hours and up to 1 day.

5. To serve, run a paring knife around the edge of each pudding. Place a dessert plate over each, invert, and tap on the bottom until the pudding releases. Reheat the caramel sauce until warm but not boiling hot and pour over each couscous pudding. Sprinkle with the chopped pistachios and serve.

Arborio Rice Pudding with Figs and Grappa *Serves 6*

Arborio rice from Italy is usually used in risotto, but it makes a superb rice pudding, especially when combined with mascarpone, a rich, tangy Italian cream cheese available in Italian specialty markets and most supermarkets. I like to use a vanilla bean instead of extract for this recipe; the dark flecks are attractive and the flavor is more intense. But you may substitute one teaspoon of vanilla if you like—stir it in when the pudding is done cooking. The dried fig and grappa compote makes this the perfect dessert to end an Italian-style winter meal. In the summer, you can skip the compote and serve the pudding with fresh figs quartered and sprinkled with a little grappa and brown sugar.

Pudding

Pinch of salt

½ cup Arborio rice

3 cups whole milk

¾ cup sugar

½ vanilla bean, split

2 large eggs

2 large egg yolks

1 cup mascarpone

Fig Compote (optional)

6 dried figs, tough stems removed

½ cup water

½ cup grappa or brandy

2 tablespoons sugar

1. To make the pudding, bring a large saucepan of water to a boil, add the salt and rice, return to a boil, and continue to boil until the rice is almost tender, about 15 minutes. Drain well.

2. Combine the boiled rice, milk, sugar, and split vanilla bean in the same saucepan (no need to wash it; just empty the water). Bring to a boil, reduce the heat to low, and simmer, uncovered, stirring frequently, until the rice is very tender and the mixture is somewhat reduced but still soupy, 20 to 25 minutes.

3. Whisk together the whole eggs and egg yolks in a medium-size bowl. Drizzle about ¼ cup of the hot rice into the eggs, whisking constantly. Drizzle in another ¼ cup of the hot rice, whisking again. Whisk the egg mixture into the pot and simmer, stirring frequently, until the pudding just begins to thicken, about 1 minute. Remove from the heat and stir in the mascarpone. Discard the vanilla bean.

4. Spoon into 6 dessert goblets or ramekins. Cover the surface of each pudding with a piece of plastic wrap to prevent a skin from forming. Refrigerate until chilled, at least 3 hours and up to 2 days.

5. To make the compote, combine the figs, water, grappa, and sugar in a small saucepan and bring to a boil. Reduce the heat to medium-low and simmer, stirring frequently, until the liquid is slightly thickened and syrupy and the fruit is softened but still holding its shape, 20 to 25 minutes. Let cool to room temperature. This will keep, refrigerated, up to 1 week; bring to room temperature before serving.

6. To serve, cut each fig into quarters, spoon 4 fig quarters and some syrup over each portion of rice pudding, and serve.

Rice Pudding Brûlée

Although one crème brûlée fanatic I know considers this an insult to his favorite dessert, for rice pudding fans there is no better way to gild the lily. You can add a crispy caramel topping to individual portions of chilled rice pudding just the way you would add it to crème brûlée.

Take your favorite rice pudding and spread it across the bottom of shallow, individual crème brûlée ramekins, filling them almost but not quite to their tops. Cover with plastic wrap and chill until very cold, at least 2 hours and up to 1 day, then sprinkle each with an ⅛-inch-thick layer of turbinado sugar, also known as "sugar in the raw." Using a small kitchen torch (available at cookware shops), begin in one corner and apply the flame to the sugar using a small circular motion, moving on when the sugar has melted and caramelized. Move the torch in this manner over the entire surface of the custard until the sugar is completely browned. Alternatively, place the ramekins on a baking sheet and set under a hot broiler until the sugar is browned, about 2 minutes. Serve immediately.

Coconut-Tapioca Pudding with Caramelized Pineapple *Serves 4*

Tapioca made with coconut milk gives this pudding a tropical flavor. Pineapple juice may be substituted for the rum, if you prefer.

Pudding

3 tablespoons quick-cooking tapioca
5 tablespoons granulated sugar
¼ teaspoon salt
2 large eggs
2½ cups canned unsweetened coconut milk, stirred well
½ cup sweetened flaked coconut
1 teaspoon vanilla extract

Pineapple Topping

2 tablespoons unsalted butter
2 tablespoons light brown sugar
1½ cups cored and peeled fresh pineapple cut into ½-inch dice (from about ¼ of a small pineapple)
¼ cup dark rum

1. To make the pudding, whisk together the tapioca, granulated sugar, salt, eggs, and coconut milk in a medium-size heavy saucepan. Let stand 10 minutes without stirring to swell the tapioca.

2. Bring the tapioca mixture to a boil, whisking constantly, then reduce the heat to medium-low and simmer, whisking constantly, for 1 minute. Remove from the heat and stir in the coconut and vanilla. Let cool for 10 minutes.

3. Spoon into 4 dessert goblets or ramekins. Cover the surface of each pudding with a piece of plastic wrap to prevent a skin from forming. Refrigerate until chilled, at least 1 hour and up to 2 days.

4. Just before serving, make the topping. Cook the butter and brown sugar in a medium-size skillet over medium heat, stirring occasionally, until the sugar dissolves. Add the pineapple and cook, stirring frequently, until lightly browned, 4 to 5 minutes. Carefully add the rum (it will bubble up) and cook, stirring frequently, until the liquid is reduced to a thick syrup, 2 to 3 minutes. Let cool slightly.

5. Spoon some of the pineapple and syrup over each portion of pudding and serve immediately.

Basmati Rice Pudding with Exotic Flavors *Serves 6*

Believe it or not, this recipe was inspired by a savory rice pilaf my husband makes and my children devour. The secret is the cardamom, which gently perfumes the mixture. A little fresh ginger spices it up, and lime zest gives it a tart flavor and flecks of color. Cornstarch, rather than egg yolks, thickens this lighter style of rice pudding without weighing it down.

Pinch of salt
½ cup basmati rice
3½ cups whole milk
2 tablespoons unsalted butter
¾ cup sugar
6 cardamom pods
One 1½-inch piece fresh ginger, peeled and
   smashed with the side of a chef's knife
1 tablespoon cornstarch
¼ teaspoon grated lime zest
½ cup peeled and diced mango (optional)

1. Bring a large saucepan of water to a boil. Add the salt and rice, return to a boil, and continue to boil until the rice is almost tender, about 15 minutes. Drain well.

2. Combine the boiled rice, 3 cups of the milk, and the butter, sugar, cardamom pods, and ginger in the same saucepan (no need to wash it; just empty the water). Bring to a boil, reduce the heat to low, and simmer, uncovered, stirring frequently, until the rice is very tender and the mixture is somewhat reduced but still soupy, 20 to 25 minutes.

3. Combine the cornstarch and remaining ½ cup of milk in a small bowl, whisking until smooth. Stir the cornstarch mixture and lime zest into the rice and simmer until the pudding just begins to thicken, about 1 minute. Remove from the heat and discard the cardamom pods and ginger.

4. Spoon into 6 dessert goblets or ramekins. Cover the surface of each pudding with a piece of plastic wrap to prevent a skin from forming. Refrigerate until chilled, at least 3 hours and up to 1 day.

5. Spoon some of the mango over each portion, if desired, just before serving.

White Chocolate Tapioca Pudding *Serves 4*

The white chocolate is subtle here—a secret ingredient that gives humble tapioca pudding an alluring flavor and an extra-creamy texture. Unless your white chocolate contains a lot of cocoa butter (only the best brands do), you won't get this effect and will just be adding extra sugar. Use a reliable brand such as Lindt or Callebaut.

3 tablespoons quick-cooking tapioca
¼ cup sugar
¼ teaspoon salt
2 large eggs
2 cups whole milk
3½ ounces white chocolate, finely chopped
1 teaspoon vanilla extract

1. Whisk the tapioca, sugar, salt, eggs, and milk together in a medium-size heavy saucepan and let stand for 5 minutes without stirring to swell the tapioca. Fill a large bowl with ice water.

2. Bring the tapioca mixture to a boil, whisking constantly, then reduce the heat to medium-low and simmer, whisking constantly, for 1 minute. Remove from the heat and stir in the white chocolate until completely melted. Stir in the vanilla.

3. Spoon into 4 dessert goblets or ramekins. Cover the surface of each pudding with a piece of plastic wrap to prevent a skin from forming. Refrigerate until chilled, at least 1 hour and up to 2 days.

CHAPTER 2

Light and Airy Mousses

Chances are, if you enjoy dipping a spoon into a rich chocolate pudding, you are also a fan of chocolate mousse. But I'd bet there are times you prefer one to the other. While you might serve chocolate pudding after a dinner of meatloaf and mashed potatoes, you'd probably save chocolate mousse for occasions when you're making rack of lamb or filet mignon.

Put simply, a mousse consists of a flavor base, such as pureed fruit or melted chocolate, lightened with whipped egg whites or whipped cream. Uncooked egg whites can be tricky and present health hazards that I'd rather not have to deal with, so I prefer to use whipped cream in my mousses. This chapter focuses on my favorite mousses— fruit fools, sabayons, frozen mousses—all lightened with whipped cream.

Fruit fools are traditional English desserts made with cooked sweetened fruit that is chilled, then folded into whipped cream. Mousses made with sabayon are among the lightest and most delicate of the bunch. Sabayon is a stovetop custard made by whipping together egg yolks, sugar, and, very often, a sweet wine such as Marsala over a pan of simmering water. The base itself is already frothy and aerated. It may be served warm or chilled and folded together with whipped cream to make a very sophisticated icebox dessert. While I was testing recipes for this book, I fell in love with molded frozen mousses. These desserts have a texture somewhere between that of a fruit fool and an ice cream. They are refreshing in the extreme and look so pretty when unmolded and garnished with fresh fruit. Even better, they can be made up to a week in advance and served straight from the freezer.

A note about portion sizes: Although mousses are light and airy, they are quite rich. As with puddings, a little goes a long way, so I've portioned out these desserts modestly.

Strawberry-Rhubarb Fool *Serves 4*

This is one of my favorite ways to use the very earliest spring fruit crops grown in my area. I love the flavor of rhubarb but could live without the stringy texture, so I puree and strain it after cooking. Because it tends to turn brownish green when cooked, I mix in some pureed strawberries for a pretty pink color.

1 pound young fresh rhubarb stalks
¾ cup plus 2 tablespoons sugar
2 tablespoons water
1 teaspoon vanilla extract
1 pint fresh strawberries, hulled and thinly
  sliced
1 cup heavy cream, chilled

1. Trim the ends from the rhubarb and cut in half lengthwise if the stalks are thick. Peel away the outer layer, removing the tough strings. Cut each stalk into 1-inch pieces.

2. Combine the rhubarb, ¾ cup of the sugar, and the water in a medium-size heavy saucepan and cook over medium heat, stirring often, until the sugar is dissolved, then continue to simmer until the rhubarb is very soft and most of the liquid has evaporated, about 10 minutes. Remove from the heat, stir in ½ teaspoon of the vanilla, and let cool slightly.

3. Transfer to a food processor, add about half of the sliced berries, and process until smooth. Push through a strainer to remove any strings and seeds. Refrigerate in an airtight container until well chilled, at least 3 hours and up to 1 week.

4. Combine the chilled puree and the remaining sliced strawberries in a large bowl.

5. In a medium-size bowl, using an electric mixer, whip together the heavy cream, the remaining 2 tablespoons of sugar, and the remaining ½ teaspoon of vanilla until it just holds stiff peaks. Gently fold into the rhubarb mixture, taking care not to deflate the cream. Cover with plastic wrap, making sure it doesn't come in contact with the fool (otherwise it may deflate), and refrigerate until ready to serve, at least 1 hour and up to 6 hours.

Fresh Apricot Fool *Serves 4*

Fresh apricots have a very short season, so when I see them in the market starting in the early summer, I grab them. I find that brief cooking intensifies their flavor. A dash of almond extract also enhances their natural perfume.

1 pound ripe apricots, pitted and each cut
  into 8 pieces
¾ cup sugar
2 tablespoons fresh lemon juice
½ teaspoon almond or vanilla extract
1 cup heavy cream, chilled
¼ cup crème fraîche or sour cream

1. Combine the apricots, all but 2 tablespoons of the sugar, and the lemon juice in a medium-size heavy saucepan and bring to a boil. Reduce the heat to medium-low, and simmer until the apricots are soft but still hold their shape, 5 to 7 minutes. Transfer to a heatproof bowl and stir in the extract. Cover with plastic wrap and refrigerate until well chilled, at least 2 hours and up to 1 week.

2. In a medium-size bowl, using an electric mixer, whip the heavy cream and remaining 2 tablespoons of sugar together until it just holds soft peaks. Add the crème fraîche and whip until it just holds stiff peaks. Gently fold the chilled apricots into the cream mixture, taking care not to deflate the cream. Cover with plastic wrap, making sure it doesn't come in contact with the fool (otherwise it may deflate), and refrigerate until ready to serve, at least 1 hour and up to 6 hours.

Simple Fruit Fools

The fruit in Strawberry-Rhubarb Fool and Fresh Apricot Fool must be cooked, but fools made with fresh berries and other soft, sweet fruits don't require this step. Raspberries, blackberries, sliced strawberries, peeled and diced mango or kiwi, and fresh figs (pulp only, skins removed) all work well.

Just combine about 2 cups of prepared fruit with ⅓ cup of sugar, or more to taste, and ½ teaspoon of vanilla extract in a medium-size bowl. Mix with a fork to release some of the juices from the fruit. Let stand about 15 minutes, stirring once or twice to make sure the sugar dissolves. Then fold the fruit into 1 cup of chilled heavy cream that has been whipped to stiff peaks with 2 tablespoons of sugar, taking care not to deflate the cream. Cover with plastic wrap, making sure it doesn't come in contact with the fool (otherwise it may deflate), and refrigerate until ready to serve, at least 1 hour and up to 6 hours.

Lemon-Thyme Mousse *Serves 6*

Lemon mousse perfumed with sprigs of fresh thyme is light, refreshing, and sophisticated. It is the perfect ending to any casual dinner party. (For straightforward lemon mousse, just leave out the thyme.)

6 large eggs

¾ cup sugar

2 teaspoons grated lemon zest

½ cup plus 2 tablespoons fresh lemon juice

1 small bunch fresh thyme

½ cup (1 stick) unsalted butter, cut into tablespoons

1 cup heavy cream, chilled

1. Whisk together the eggs, sugar, and lemon zest in a medium-size heavy saucepan until smooth. Add the lemon juice, thyme, and butter and cook over medium heat, whisking constantly, until thickened, 7 to 9 minutes. Do not allow the mixture to come to a boil. Pour through a fine mesh strainer into a heatproof bowl. Cover the surface while still hot with plastic wrap and refrigerate until cold and thick, at least 3 hours and up to 3 days.

2. In a medium-size bowl, using an electric mixer, whip the heavy cream until stiff peaks form. Gently fold into the chilled lemon curd with a rubber spatula, being careful not to deflate the cream. Scrape into 6 dessert goblets or ramekins. Cover with plastic wrap, making sure it doesn't come in contact with the mousse (otherwise it might deflate), and refrigerate until well chilled, at least 3 hours and up to 1 day.

 ## Properly Whipped Cream

Crucial to every recipe in this chapter is properly whipped cream. Whipped to the right consistency, heavy cream will lighten a mousse and give it a smooth, soft texture. Whipped improperly, it may make a mousse heavy and lumpy. Follow these tips for the best results:

1. Make sure the cream, bowl, and beaters are well chilled before whipping. Very cold cream whips up higher than warmer cream.

2. Whip the cream until it just holds stiff peaks. This means that when the whisk or beater is lifted up from the cream, the cream forms a point that stands upright and doesn't flop over.

Underwhipping the cream will cheat your mousse of needed air.

3. Take care not to overwhip. Properly whipped cream is smooth and shiny. Overwhipped cream begins to form lumps and ultimately separates into liquid and blobs of butterfat. To ensure this doesn't happen, you might consider finishing the whipping by hand. An electric mixer can very quickly take cream from the soft peak stage to the lumpy stage. When your cream begins to hold soft, floppy peaks, turn off the mixer and continue to whisk by hand until stiff, smooth peaks are achieved. Whipped cream will keep for several hours in the refrigerator. Rewhisk it a few times before serving.

Chocolate-Honey Mousse *Serves 6*

Chocolate mousse recipes are a dime a dozen, so I debated whether to include one here. But this simple variation is so delicious and unusual that I've decided to let it represent the category in this book. Any honey will do, but if you have a particular favorite, by all means let it lend its character to the mixture. If you see extra-bittersweet chocolate (Scharffen Berger and Valrhona make chocolate with a higher percentage of chocolate liquor—about 70 percent—than is customary), you might want to give it a try. The more intense flavor of this very dark chocolate contrasts well with the sweetness of the honey.

7 ounces bittersweet (not unsweetened) chocolate, finely chopped
1¼ cups heavy cream, chilled
¼ cup honey
6 Chocolate Cups (see page 39; optional)

1. Bring 2 inches of water to a bare simmer in a medium-size saucepan. Combine the chocolate, ¼ cup of the cream, and the honey in a stainless-steel bowl big enough to rest on top of the saucepan and set over the simmering water, making sure it doesn't touch the water. Heat, whisking occasionally, until the chocolate is completely melted, then let cool slightly until just warm to the touch.

2. In a medium-size bowl, using an electric mixer, whip the remaining 1 cup of heavy cream until it just holds stiff peaks. Gently fold into the cooled chocolate mixture, taking care not to deflate the cream. Spoon into 6 dessert goblets or the Chocolate Cups, if desired. Cover the goblets with plastic wrap, making sure it doesn't come in contact with the mousse, otherwise it might deflate. (If using Chocolate Cups, do not wrap in plastic.) Refrigerate for at least 3 hours and up to 1 day before serving.

Molded Peach-Raspberry Mousse *Serves 6 to 8*

This dessert can be either refrigerated or frozen. Refrigerated, it is a mousse that holds its shape because of the added gelatin. Frozen, it becomes more like ice cream. Either way, it is an easy and unusual way to showcase late summer fruit.

1 envelope unflavored gelatin

3 tablespoons cold water

4 medium-size ripe peaches, peeled, pitted, and sliced

½ cup plus 2 tablespoons sugar

1 cup fresh raspberries

1½ cups heavy cream, chilled

1 tablespoon peach schnapps (optional)

1 teaspoon vanilla extract

1. Sprinkle the gelatin over the water in a small bowl and let soften for 2 minutes.

2. Combine the peaches and sugar in a medium-size heavy saucepan over medium-low heat and cook, stirring a few times, until the sugar dissolves and the mixture is warm to the touch, 3 to 5 minutes. Transfer to a food processor, add the gelatin mixture, and process until smooth. Transfer to a large bowl and gently stir in the raspberries. Let cool to room temperature.

3. Combine the heavy cream, peach schnapps, if using, and vanilla in a medium-size bowl and, using an electric mixer, whip until stiff peaks form. Gently fold into the peach-raspberry mixture, taking care not to deflate the cream, then scrape into a 1-quart ring mold or bowl. Cover with plastic wrap and refrigerate until completely set, at least 6 hours and up to 1 day, or freeze for up to 1 week.

4. To serve, place the mold in hot water for 15 to 20 seconds (30 seconds if frozen). Place a serving platter over the mold, invert, and tap gently to unmold. If the mousse has been refrigerated, slice and serve immediately. If it has been frozen, allow to sit on the counter for 30 minutes before slicing and serving.

White Chocolate and Orange Mousse *Serves 6*

This is an adaptation of Roland Mesnier's white chocolate mousse. Roland was the pastry chef at the White House for 25 years, and he served this mousse to five presidents and innumerable dignitaries. The secret is the large quantity of orange liqueur, which not only flavors the mousse but also cuts the sweetness and richness of the cream and chocolate. It's very important that the chocolate is still a little warm when folded into the cream. This way it will mix well before it begins to harden. Garnish with candied orange peel, curls of orange zest, or white chocolate, if you'd like.

8 ounces best-quality white chocolate
1 cup heavy cream, chilled
¼ cup Grand Marnier or other orange liqueur
6 Chocolate Cups (see opposite; optional)

1. In a medium-size saucepan, bring 2 inches of water to a bare simmer. Place the chocolate in a stainless-steel bowl big enough to rest on top of the saucepan and set it over the pan, making sure it doesn't touch the water. Heat, whisking occasionally, until completely melted. Let cool slightly, until just warm to the touch.

2. In a medium-size bowl, using an electric mixer, whip the heavy cream until it just holds stiff peaks. Gently but quickly fold the whipped cream and Grand Marnier into the chocolate all at once, taking care not to deflate the cream. Spoon into 6 dessert goblets or the Chocolate Cups, if desired. Cover the goblets with plastic wrap, making sure it doesn't touch the mousse, otherwise it might deflate. (If using Chocolate Cups, do not wrap in plastic.) Refrigerate for at least 3 hours and up to 1 day before serving.

Hazelnut Mousse *Serves 6*

This simple mousse is made with Nutella, the hazelnut and chocolate spread so popular in Europe. It's especially good when frozen, when it resembles the *gianduia* gelato served in tiny cups at all the wonderful ice cream parlors in Italy. Don't skip the sour cream, which gives the dessert some depth. To skin hazelnuts, place them on a baking sheet in a preheated 350°F oven for 10 minutes. Wrap the hot nuts in a clean kitchen towel and allow them to steam for 10 minutes. Then rub them inside the towel to remove the skins.

1 cup heavy cream, chilled

2 tablespoons Frangelico or other hazelnut liqueur

¼ cup full-fat (not low- or nonfat) sour cream

1 cup Nutella

¼ cup hazelnuts, toasted, skinned (see headnote), and finely chopped

6 Chocolate Cups (see below; optional)

1. Combine the cream and Frangelico in a medium-size bowl and, using an electric mixer, whip until it just holds soft peaks. Add the sour cream and whip until it just holds stiff peaks.

2. In a large bowl, stir together the Nutella and about one-fourth of the whipped cream. Gently fold in the remaining whipped cream and the nuts, being careful not to deflate the cream. Spoon into 6 dessert goblets or Chocolate Cups, if desired. Cover the goblets with plastic wrap, making sure it doesn't touch the mousse, otherwise it might deflate. (If using Chocolate Cups, do not wrap in plastic.) Refrigerate for at least 3 hours and up to 1 day before serving.

 ## Making Chocolate Cups

I just love the idea of serving a mousse in an edible chocolate cup. You can buy chocolate cups in gourmet shops, but they are fun and very simple to make at home.

Inflate 12 or so small balloons (blown up, they should be no larger than the size of a baseball). In a medium-size saucepan, bring 2 inches of water to a bare simmer. Place 8 ounces semisweet or bittersweet chocolate in a stainless-steel bowl big enough to rest on top of the saucepan and set it over the pan, making sure it doesn't touch the water. Heat, whisking occasionally, until completely melted. Let cool slightly, until just warm to the touch. Dip each balloon into the melted chocolate about halfway. Lift it from the chocolate and set on parchment paper, chocolate side down. The excess chocolate will drip down the sides of the balloon to form a base. When the chocolate is completely set, carefully pierce the balloon with a paring knife and peel it away from the chocolate cup. Chocolate cups will keep, covered, at room temperature, for up to 2 weeks.

Champagne Sabayon Mousse *Serves 6*

Sabayon is absolutely the lightest and most delicate stovetop custard you can make. Often it is served warm, poured over ripe berries or sautéed fruit. When allowed to cool and combined with whipped cream, sabayon makes an ethereal mousse. My favorite is flavored with champagne. Depending on your preference and the time of year, you may either refrigerate or freeze it. See below for some terrific variations.

6 large egg yolks
⅔ cup plus 2 tablespoons sugar
1 cup champagne or sparkling wine
1 cup heavy cream, chilled

1. In a medium-size saucepan, bring 2 inches of water to a bare simmer. In a stainless-steel bowl big enough to rest on top of the saucepan, whisk together the egg yolks and ⅔ cup of the sugar until foamy, then set over the pan of water without letting it touch the water. Whisk constantly until it begins to thicken, about 1 minute. Slowly whisk in the champagne and continue to cook, whisking constantly, until warm to the touch, pale yellow, and about triple in volume, 5 to 7 minutes. Let cool to room temperature.

2. In a medium-size bowl, using an electric mixer, whip together the heavy cream and the remaining 2 tablespoons of sugar until it just holds stiff peaks (be careful not to overwhip). Gently fold into the cooled sabayon with a rubber spatula, being careful not to deflate the cream. Gently scrape into 6 dessert goblets or ramekins and cover with plastic wrap, making sure it doesn't touch the mousse (otherwise it might deflate). Refrigerate until well chilled, at least 3 hours and up to 1 day.

Playing Around with Sabayon Mousses

Use the recipe for Champagne Sabayon Mousse as the foundation for making these variations:

- **Lemon Sabayon Mousse**: Substitute 1 teaspoon of grated lemon zest and 6 tablespoons of fresh lemon juice for the champagne. Serve with fresh blueberries.
- **Marsala Sabayon Mousse**: Substitute ⅓ cup of Marsala for the champagne. Serve with sweetened sliced strawberries.
- **Armagnac- or Brandy-Spiked Sabayon Mousse**: Substitute ⅓ cup of Armagnac or brandy for the champagne. Serve with sliced plums, brandied prunes, or poached pears.
- **Vin Santo Sabayon Mousse**: Substitute ⅓ cup of Vin Santo for the champagne. Serve with almond biscotti.

Sambuca and Espresso Sabayon Mousse *Serves 6*

For my entire life, I've been a "chocolate" person, until about a year ago, when I developed a sudden mania for black licorice. Realizing that I had no licorice-flavored items in my repertoire, I was determined to enjoy my new obsession as a real dessert. Remembering the classic Italian combination of sambuca and espresso, I thought I'd try to concoct a sabayon mousse flavored with both. After some experimenting, here it is. Turbinado sugar (otherwise known as "sugar in the raw") mixed with espresso powder makes a very simple, crunchy topping.

2 teaspoons instant espresso powder

1 tablespoon boiling water

6 large egg yolks

⅔ cup granulated sugar

⅓ cup sambuca or other anise-flavored liqueur

1¼ cups heavy cream, chilled

3 tablespoons turbinado sugar

1. Place 1½ teaspoons of the espresso powder in a small bowl and stir in the boiling water to dissolve. Set aside to cool.

2. In a medium-size saucepan, bring 2 inches of water to a bare simmer. In a stainless-steel bowl big enough to rest on top of the saucepan, whisk together the egg yolks, granulated sugar, and sambuca until foamy, then set over the pan without letting it touch the water. Whisk constantly until warm to the touch, slightly thickened, and lighter in color, 6 to 8 minutes. Remove from the heat, whisk in the espresso mixture, and beat, using an electric mixer, until completely cool, 7 to 10 minutes. Clean and dry the beaters.

3. In a medium-size bowl, using the electric mixer, whip the cream until it just holds stiff peaks (be careful not to overwhip). Gently fold it into the cooled sabayon with a rubber spatula, being careful not to deflate the cream. Gently scrape into 6 dessert goblets or ramekins and cover with plastic wrap, making sure it doesn't touch the mousse (otherwise it might deflate). Refrigerate until well chilled, at least 3 hours and up to 1 day.

4. When ready to serve, mix together the turbinado sugar and the remaining ½ teaspoon of espresso powder. Sprinkle some over each sabayon portion and serve immediately.

Frozen Margarita Mousse *Serves 6 to 8*

This is a light and lovely summer dessert. Garnish with fresh raspberries or mandarin orange slices for a beautiful presentation. If you'd like, you can spoon it into margarita glasses rimmed with salt (or sugar, if you prefer) and refrigerate for several hours rather than freezing. In that case, garnish each with a twist of lime.

1 envelope unflavored gelatin

3 tablespoons cold water

¾ cup sugar

½ cup fresh lime juice

¼ cup fresh lemon juice

2 teaspoons grated lime zest

¼ cup tequila

2 tablespoons triple sec

1½ cups heavy cream, chilled

1. Sprinkle the gelatin over the water in a small bowl and let soften for 2 minutes.

2. Combine the sugar and citrus juices in a medium-size heavy saucepan over medium heat and cook, stirring a few times, until the sugar dissolves and the mixture is warm to the touch. Remove from the heat and whisk in the gelatin mixture, then whisk in the lime zest, tequila, and triple sec. Place over a large bowl of ice water and let stand, whisking occasionally, until it is chilled and begins to thicken but is not yet solidifying, 15 to 20 minutes.

3. In a large bowl, using an electric mixer, whip the cream until it just holds stiff peaks. Gently fold the cooled tequila-lime mixture into the whipped cream, taking care not to deflate the cream, then scrape into a 1-quart ring mold or bowl. Cover with plastic wrap and freeze until completely set, at least 6 hours and up to 1 day.

4. To serve, place the mold in hot water for 30 seconds. Place a serving platter over the mold, invert, and tap gently to unmold. Let stand on the counter for 30 minutes, then slice and serve.

Maple-Bourbon Sabayon Mousse with Chocolate-Maple Sauce *Serves 6*

Dark rum may be substituted for the bourbon, if you like. The sauce is one of my favorites and terrific over vanilla or coffee ice cream if you don't have time to make the sabayon mousse.

Maple-Bourbon Sabayon Mousse

6 large egg yolks

½ cup plus 2 tablespoons pure maple syrup

2 tablespoons bourbon

1¼ cups heavy cream, chilled

Chocolate-Maple Sauce

½ cup pure maple syrup

1 ounce unsweetened chocolate, coarsely chopped

1 tablespoon unsalted butter

¼ cup finely chopped walnuts

1. To make the mousse, in a medium-size saucepan, bring 2 inches of water to a bare simmer. In a stainless-steel bowl big enough to rest on top of the saucepan, whisk together the egg yolks and maple syrup until foamy, then set over the pan without letting it touch the water. Whisk constantly until warm to the touch, slightly thickened, and lighter in color, 6 to 8 minutes. Remove from the heat and beat, using an electric mixer, until completely cool, 7 to 10 minutes. Stir in the bourbon. Wash and dry the beaters.

2. In a medium-size bowl, using the mixer, whip the heavy cream until it just holds stiff peaks (be careful not to overwhip). Gently fold into the cooled sabayon with a rubber spatula, being careful not to deflate the cream. Gently scrape into 6 dessert goblets or ramekins and cover with plastic wrap, making sure it doesn't touch the mousse (otherwise it might deflate). Refrigerate until well chilled, at least 3 hours and up to 1 day.

3. To make the sauce, combine the maple syrup and chocolate in a small heavy saucepan over medium heat and cook, whisking constantly, until just simmering. Remove from the heat and whisk in the butter. Stir in the nuts. Use immediately or keep in an airtight container at room temperature for up to 1 week and reheat briefly before using. Spoon the warm sauce over the chilled cups of mousse and serve immediately.

Frozen Piña Colada Mousse *Serves 6 to 8*

This is delightful on a summer night, with or without the rum.

1 envelope unflavored gelatin

3 tablespoons cold water

One 6-ounce can pineapple juice

One 15-ounce can cream of coconut (such as Coco Lopez brand), stirred well

¼ cup light rum (optional)

1⅓ cups heavy cream, chilled

1. Sprinkle the gelatin over the water in a small bowl and let soften for 2 minutes.

2. Combine the pineapple juice and cream of coconut in a medium-size heavy saucepan over medium heat and cook until warm to the touch. Remove from the heat and whisk in the gelatin mixture. Whisk in the rum, if using. Place over a large bowl of ice water and let stand, whisking occasionally, until it is chilled and begins to thicken but is not yet solidifying, 15 to 20 minutes.

3. In a large bowl, using an electric mixer, whip the cream until it just holds stiff peaks. Gently fold the cooled pineapple-coconut mixture into the whipped cream, taking care not to deflate the cream, then scrape into a 1-quart ring mold or bowl. Cover with plastic wrap and freeze until completely set, at least 6 hours and up to 1 day.

4. To serve, place the mold in hot water for 30 seconds. Place a serving platter over the mold, invert, and tap gently to unmold. Let stand on the counter for 30 minutes, then slice and serve.

Peanut Butter Mousse Sandwiches *Makes 12 sandwiches*

These look like miniature ice cream sandwiches, but the peanut butter mousse filling is a little lighter and easier to work with than ice cream. Spreading melted chocolate on the inside of one of the chocolate wafer cookies is a simple way to give these treats an intense chocolate flavor.

½ cup semisweet chocolate chips
24 Nabisco Famous Chocolate Wafer Cookies
2 tablespoons finely chopped salted peanuts
¾ cup heavy cream, chilled
2 tablespoons confectioners' sugar
½ teaspoon vanilla extract
½ cup smooth peanut butter

1. Line a rimmed baking sheet with parchment paper.

2. In a medium-size saucepan, bring 2 inches of water to a bare simmer. Place the chocolate chips in a stainless-steel bowl big enough to rest on top of the saucepan and set over the pan, making sure it doesn't touch the water. Heat, whisking occasionally, until completely melted.

3. Use a small offset spatula to spread some of the melted chocolate on the flat side of 12 of the wafer cookies. Place the cookies, chocolate side up, on the prepared baking sheet. Sprinkle each cookie with ½ teaspoon of the chopped peanuts and set aside.

4. Combine the cream, confectioners' sugar, and vanilla in a medium-size bowl and, using an electric mixer, whip until it just holds stiff peaks.

5. Place the peanut butter in a small bowl and stir in about one-fourth of the whipped cream to lighten it. Gently fold the peanut butter mixture back into the rest of the whipped cream, taking care not to deflate it. Spoon heaping tablespoonfuls of the peanut butter mousse onto the remaining 12 wafer cookies. Top each one with a chocolate-covered wafer cookie, chocolate side facing in. Return the cookies to the baking sheet, cover with plastic wrap, and freeze until firm, at least 1 hour and up to 2 days. Serve straight from the freezer or let stand on the countertop for 15 minutes to soften before serving.

White Chocolate–Mint Mousse Sandwiches *Makes 12 sandwiches*

Here is one of my favorite flavor combinations—mint and white chocolate—whipped into a mousse and sandwiched between chocolate wafer cookies. To dress them up, you may dip the frozen sandwiches halfway into melted bittersweet chocolate.

8 ounces best-quality white chocolate, finely chopped
1 cup heavy cream, chilled
½ teaspoon peppermint extract
1 or 2 drops green food coloring (optional)
24 Nabisco Famous Chocolate Wafer Cookies
8 ounces bittersweet chocolate (optional), finely chopped

1. Line a rimmed baking sheet with parchment paper.

2. In a medium-size saucepan, bring 2 inches of water to a bare simmer. Place the white chocolate in a stainless-steel bowl big enough to rest on top of the saucepan and set over the pan, making sure it doesn't touch the water. Heat, whisking occasionally, until completely melted. Let cool until just warm to the touch.

3. In a medium-size bowl, using an electric mixer, whip together the heavy cream, peppermint extract, and food coloring, if using, until it just holds stiff peaks. Gently but quickly fold into the white chocolate all at once, taking care not to deflate the cream. Spoon heaping tablespoonfuls of the mousse onto 12 of the wafer cookies. Top each one with another wafer cookie. Place the cookies on the prepared baking sheet, cover with plastic wrap, and freeze until firm, at least 1 hour and up to 2 days. You can eat these directly from the freezer.

4. To dip the cookie sandwiches into chocolate, if desired, melt the bittersweet chocolate in a stainless-steel bowl set over simmering water, stirring until smooth. Let cool until just warm to the touch. Remove the sandwiches from the freezer and dip half of each cookie into the chocolate. Scrape any excess off the cookie and back into the bowl. Return the cookies to the baking sheet, freeze until the chocolate is firm, and serve, or cover with plastic wrap and freeze for up to 2 weeks.

Gingersnap and Ginger Mousse Sandwiches *Makes 12 sandwiches*

If you can find them, the thinner type of gingersnaps made by Swedish Kitchen (I buy mine at the supermarket, and they are available at many gourmet and specialty foods shops) are especially good here. And, of course, homemade cookies are always terrific!

One 8-ounce package cream cheese, softened
½ cup confectioners' sugar
¼ teaspoon ground cinnamon
¼ teaspoon vanilla extract
¼ cup minced crystallized ginger
½ teaspoon grated lemon zest
¾ cup heavy cream, chilled
24 gingersnap cookies
8 ounces white chocolate (optional), finely
  chopped

1. Line a rimmed baking sheet with parchment paper.

2. Place the cream cheese in a medium-size bowl and, using an electric mixer, beat until fluffy. Add the confectioners' sugar, cinnamon, and vanilla and beat until well combined. Stir in the ginger and lemon zest. Wash and dry the beaters.

3. In a small bowl, using the mixer, whip the heavy cream until it just holds stiff peaks. Gently fold into the cream cheese mixture, being careful not to deflate the cream. Spoon heaping tablespoonfuls of the mousse onto 12 gingersnaps. Top each one with another ginger-snap. Place on the prepared baking sheet, cover with plastic wrap, and freeze until firm, at least 1 hour and up to 2 days.

4. To dip the cookie sandwiches in white chocolate, if desired, bring 2 inches of water to a bare simmer in a medium-size saucepan. Place the chocolate in a stainless-steel bowl big enough to rest on top of the saucepan and set over the pan, making sure it doesn't touch the water. Heat, whisking occasionally, until completely melted. Let cool until just warm to the touch.

5. Remove the sandwiches from the freezer and dip half of each into the chocolate. Scrape any excess off the cookie and back into the bowl. Return the cookies to the baking sheet, freeze until the chocolate is firm, and serve, or cover with plastic wrap and freeze for up to 2 weeks.

CHAPTER 3

Dessert in a Glass: Icebox Parfaits

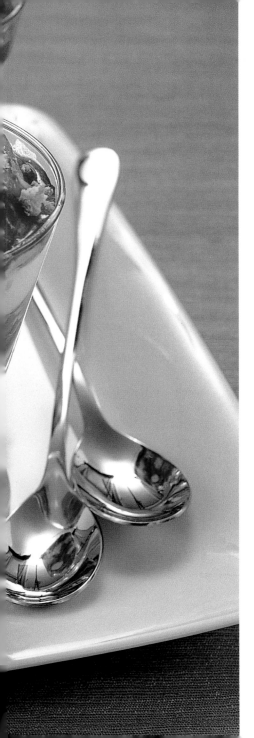

When I want to make a simple, satisfying dinner that nonetheless contains an interesting mixture of textures and flavors, I look no further than the sandwich, a layering of ingredients that can be as simple and streamlined as grilled cheese or as Baroque as a hero with the works. When I want to make a simple, satisfying *dessert* that nonetheless contains an interesting mixture of textures and flavors, I look no further than the parfait. The parfait is the sandwich of desserts, a layered creation that can be as spare as some sliced strawberries alternating with bands of sweetened ricotta cheese or as sweet, rich, and over the top as banana caramel pudding with whipped cream and crushed vanilla wafers.

Like sandwiches, parfait recipes are casual and endlessly adaptable. There is no limit to the number of parfaits you can create by layering fruit, whipped cream, pudding, mousse, nuts, crushed cookies and candy, and ice cream in various combinations according to taste (see pages 139–140 for ice cream parfaits). That said, more is not necessarily better when it comes to designing a parfait. I prefer parfaits in which the ingredients are thoughtfully combined to complement each other, rather than those that contain everything but the proverbial kitchen sink. Loading on the extras will not necessarily make for a better dessert. As with a good sandwich, the ingredients should be distinct, but the whole should always be more than the sum of the parts. If you find yourself pushing aside one layer to get to the next, rather than enjoying the dessert as a whole, then something's not right. A properly made parfait will compel you to scoop a little bit of each layer onto your spoon with every bite, to get the most enjoyment out of the combinations.

The parfait is one of my favorite icebox desserts for entertaining. While most are not much more difficult to make than any of the recipes for simple puddings in Chapter 1 (and some are quite a bit easier), they do demand an admiring audience. Layering yummy-looking ingredients in a glass instantly creates visual interest. They are also nice for entertaining because they are made up as individual servings. Presenting each guest with his or her own gem of a dessert is a show-stopping way to end dinner. And since you've made the desserts ahead of time, all you have to do is pull them out of the fridge at the last minute.

Sweet Ricotta and Strawberry Parfaits *Serves 4*

Supermarket ricotta cheese works fine here, but there's nothing like the sweet creaminess of fresh ricotta, available in specialty markets and Italian foods stores. A little splash of balsamic vinegar brightens the flavor of the berries.

One 15- or 16-ounce container whole milk ricotta cheese
6 tablespoons confectioners' sugar
1 cup heavy cream, chilled
1 pint fresh strawberries, hulled and thinly sliced
3 tablespoons granulated sugar
1 tablespoon balsamic vinegar

1. Line a small colander or mesh strainer with several layers of paper towels and set over a bowl. Spread the ricotta on top and let drain until thickened and creamy, about 1 hour.

2. Transfer the ricotta to a medium-size bowl and stir in 4 tablespoons of the confectioners' sugar until well combined.

3. In a large bowl, using an electric mixer, whip together the cream and the remaining 2 tablespoons of confectioners' sugar until it just holds stiff peaks. Gently fold the ricotta into the whipped cream, taking care not to deflate the cream.

4. In another medium-size bowl, gently toss together the strawberries, granulated sugar, and balsamic vinegar and let stand for 5 minutes, stirring once or twice, until the sugar dissolves.

5. Spoon some of the strawberries into each of 4 parfait glasses. Spoon some of the ricotta-cream mixture on top of the berries. Add another layer of strawberries and another layer of the ricotta mixture, using up the remainder of each. Cover with plastic wrap and refrigerate for at least 1 hour and up to 6 hours before serving.

Blackberry and Cream Cheese Mousse Parfaits *Serves 4*

This is a kind of cheesecake in reverse, with the creamy mousse going into the parfait glass first and the ground graham crackers sprinkled on at the last minute as a topping. It's a good way to use delicious but expensive blackberries without breaking the bank, because you need less than a pint for 4 portions.

3 cups fresh blackberries

3 tablespoons granulated sugar

1 tablespoon fresh lemon juice

One 8-ounce package cream cheese, at room temperature

½ cup confectioners' sugar

6 tablespoons full-fat (not low- or nonfat) sour cream

1 teaspoon grated lemon zest

½ teaspoon vanilla extract

½ cup heavy cream, chilled

2 whole graham crackers

1 tablespoon unsalted butter

1. Combine the blackberries, 2 tablespoons of the granulated sugar, and the lemon juice in a medium-size bowl, mashing about half of the berries to release their juices. Let stand, stirring a few times, to dissolve the sugar, about 10 minutes.

2. In another medium-size bowl, using an electric mixer, combine the cream cheese and confectioners' sugar until smooth. Beat in the sour cream, lemon zest, and vanilla. Wash and dry the beaters.

3. In a small bowl, using the mixer, whip the heavy cream until it just holds stiff peaks. Gently fold into the cream cheese mixture, taking care not to deflate the cream. Divide the mousse among 4 sundae dishes or parfait glasses and spoon the berries on top. Cover with plastic wrap and refrigerate for at least 1 hour and up to 6 hours before serving.

4. When ready to serve, combine the graham crackers and remaining 1 tablespoon of granulated sugar in a food processor and process until finely ground. In a small bowl, melt the butter in the microwave. Add the melted butter to the graham crackers and pulse once or twice to combine. Sprinkle the topping on the parfaits and serve immediately.

Mascarpone and Cherry Parfaits *Serves 4*

This is an absolutely sensational dessert that requires nothing more than a small amount of mixing and chopping. The portions are small because the combination is so rich. Any type of biscotti may be used here; I am partial to a locally made cookie studded with almonds and pistachios.

8 ounces mascarpone

1 tablespoon sweet Marsala wine

¼ cup heavy cream, chilled

2 tablespoons confectioners' sugar

6 store-bought biscotti cookies, coarsely chopped

½ cup best-quality sour cherry preserves

1. In a medium-size bowl, using an electric mixer, beat the mascarpone, Marsala, heavy cream, and confectioners' sugar until smooth.

2. Divide the chopped biscotti among 4 parfait glasses. Spoon the cherries over the biscotti, then top with the mascarpone mixture. Cover with plastic wrap and refrigerate for at least 30 minutes and up to 3 hours before serving.

Create Your Own Parfait

If you are crafty or artistically inclined, designing a parfait that contains your own favorite flavors and textures is a tasty way to satisfy your creative yearnings *and* your sweet tooth. Start with the following puddings and mousses, then let your imagination dictate the other layering ingredients:

- **Spiked Butterscotch Pudding** (page 16)
- **Chocolate Pudding for Beginners** (page 17)
- **Cinnamon-Raisin Rice Pudding** (page 21)
- **Basmati Rice Pudding with Exotic Flavors** (page 28)
- **White Chocolate Tapioca Pudding** (page 29)
- **Lemon-Thyme Mousse** (page 34)

- **Chocolate-Honey Mousse** (page 35)
- **White Chocolate and Orange Mousse** (page 38)
- **Champagne Sabayon Mousse** (page 40)
- **Sambuca and Espresso Sabayon Mousse** (page 41)

For the other layers, consider fresh and dried fruits, crumbled cookies, chopped nuts, and whipped cream when deciding on your scheme. The watchword is restraint. Just the way fashion gurus advise removing one accessory (the scarf, the necklace, the belt) before leaving the house, consider removing one layering ingredient from your list, if that list numbers more than three or four, and saving it for next time.

Black Bottom Pudding Parfaits *Serves 4*

This one is for people who just can't choose between chocolate and butterscotch pudding!

3 tablespoons unsalted butter

½ cup firmly packed dark brown sugar

⅛ teaspoon salt

3 tablespoons cornstarch

2 cups half-and-half

1 teaspoon vanilla extract

2 ounces bittersweet chocolate, finely chopped

¼ cup graham cracker or chocolate wafer cookie crumbs

1. Combine the butter, brown sugar, and salt in a medium-size heavy saucepan and cook over low heat, whisking, until the butter melts and the sugar dissolves.

2. Whisk together the cornstarch and ½ cup of the half-and-half in a small bowl.

3. Add the remaining 1½ cups of half-and-half to the saucepan with the butter and sugar mixture and whisk until combined. Add the cornstarch mixture, stir to combine, and turn the heat to medium-high. Cook, whisking, until it thickens, 3 to 4 minutes. Whisk in the vanilla. Pour 1 cup of the butterscotch pudding into a large heatproof measuring cup and set aside.

4. Add the chocolate to the saucepan with the remaining pudding and stir quickly until smooth. Divide the chocolate pudding among 4 parfait glasses. Sprinkle 1 tablespoon of graham cracker crumbs over each parfait, then top each glass with ¼ cup of the butterscotch pudding. Cover with plastic wrap and refrigerate until completely set, at least 3 hours and up to 1 day.

Parfait Presentation

A not inconsiderable pleasure of the parfait is the way it looks in a parfait glass. But it's not necessary to go out and buy parfait glasses to make any of the recipes in this chapter. Other types of glassware work just fine, and you probably have several suitable choices in your cabinet right now. Just be sure to use clear glass (colored or opaque would defeat the purpose) and use common sense to judge which of your glasses will be right for a particular recipe. I alternate my parfait glasses with sundae dishes, martini glasses, margarita glasses, small compotes, jelly jars, old-fashioned glasses, and highballs. I like to pretend I am a food stylist, trolling outlet stores and tag sales for unusual dessert glasses. Putting them in rotation helps me justify this fantasy life and lends variety to my table settings.

Tapioca and Rhubarb Compote Parfaits *Serves 4*

I love tart rhubarb compote layered with creamy tapioca pudding and enriched with a little crème fraîche (sour cream may be substituted, if you prefer). This is the perfect springtime dessert, when everyone starts to crave fresh fruit and local rhubarb is just coming into the market.

Rhubarb Compote

1 pound fresh rhubarb stalks, ends trimmed, strings removed, and cut into ½-inch pieces

2 tablespoons fresh orange juice

½ cup plus 2 tablespoons sugar

¼ teaspoon ground cinnamon

¼ teaspoon ground ginger

Tapioca Pudding

3 tablespoons quick-cooking tapioca

5 tablespoons sugar

¼ teaspoon salt

2 large eggs

2 cups whole milk

1 teaspoon vanilla extract

½ cup crème fraîche

Crystallized ginger for garnish (optional)

1. To make the rhubarb compote, combine the rhubarb, orange juice, sugar, cinnamon, and ginger in a medium-size heavy saucepan and bring to a boil. Reduce the heat to low and cook at a bare simmer, stirring occasionally, until the rhubarb is tender but not yet falling apart, 7 to 10 minutes. Transfer to a heatproof bowl and let cool to room temperature. Cover with plastic wrap and refrigerate until cool and thick, at least 1 hour and up to 1 day.

2. To make the tapioca pudding, whisk together the tapioca, sugar, salt, and eggs in a medium-size heavy saucepan, then whisk in the milk. Let stand for 5 minutes without stirring to swell the tapioca. Fill a large bowl with ice water.

3. Bring the tapioca to a boil, whisking constantly. Reduce the heat to medium-low and simmer, whisking constantly, for 1 minute. Stir in the vanilla. Place the saucepan in the bowl of ice water and let stand, stirring once or twice, until thickened and cooled to room temperature, about 5 minutes. Stir in the crème fraîche.

4. Spoon some of the cold rhubarb into 4 sundae dishes or large martini glasses. Spoon some of the warm tapioca on top, then add another layer of rhubarb and another layer of tapioca, using both up. Cover with plastic wrap and refrigerate for at least 1 hour and up to 6 hours before serving. Garnish with crystallized ginger, if desired.

Lemon Gelatin Parfaits *Serves 6*

I developed a version of this recipe years ago for a book I wrote called *Just Add Water*. None of the recipes in the book required any knowledge of cooking other than how to bring water to a boil. It just goes to show how a few simple ingredients minimally handled can add up to a fun, fresh, pretty dessert.

3 envelopes unflavored gelatin
3¾ cups cold water
1½ cups plus 3 tablespoons sugar
1½ cups fresh lemon juice
1 teaspoon grated lemon zest
¾ cup heavy cream, chilled
6 sprigs fresh mint for garnish (optional)

1. In a small bowl, sprinkle the gelatin over ½ cup of the cold water and let soften for 2 minutes. Meanwhile, combine the remaining 3¼ cups of water, 1½ cups of the sugar, and the lemon juice and zest in a medium-size heavy saucepan and bring to a boil. Turn off the heat and whisk in the gelatin mixture for 1 minute to dissolve any lumps. Transfer to a heatproof medium-size bowl, let cool, then cover with plastic wrap and refrigerate until firm, at least 6 hours and up to 1 day.

2. In a medium-size bowl, using an electric mixer, whip together the heavy cream and the remaining 3 tablespoons of sugar until it holds stiff peaks.

3. Spoon half the lemon gelatin into 6 goblets or sundae glasses. Top with half the whipped cream. Divide the remaining gelatin among the goblets and top with the remaining whipped cream. Garnish with the mint sprigs, if desired, and serve. (Do not store in the refrigerator for longer than 30 minutes.)

Butterscotch Tapioca and Pecan-Coffee Crunch Parfaits *Serves 4*

My husband loves tapioca above all other pudding desserts, and pecans above all other nuts, so I developed this one for him. I enjoy the strong flavor of coffee with the pecans, but for a milder dessert, leave out the espresso powder.

⅔ cup pecans

½ cup plus 2 tablespoons heavy cream, chilled

4 tablespoons granulated sugar

2 teaspoons instant espresso powder (optional)

¼ teaspoon salt

3 tablespoons quick-cooking tapioca

5 tablespoons firmly packed dark brown sugar

2 large eggs

2 cups whole milk

1 tablespoon unsalted butter

1 teaspoon vanilla extract

1. Combine the pecans, 2 tablespoons of the heavy cream, 2 tablespoons of the granulated sugar, the espresso powder, if using, and ⅛ teaspoon of salt in a small heavy saucepan and cook over medium heat, stirring, until the cream has almost entirely evaporated, about 3 minutes. Turn the nuts onto a parchment- or waxed paper–lined baking sheet, let cool completely, and finely chop.

2. In a medium-size heavy saucepan, whisk together the tapioca, brown sugar, remaining ⅛ teaspoon of salt, and the eggs, then whisk in the milk. Let stand for 5 minutes without stirring to swell the tapioca. Fill a large bowl with ice water.

3. Bring the tapioca to a boil, whisking constantly. Reduce the heat to medium-low and simmer, whisking constantly, for 1 minute. Stir in the butter and vanilla, then place the saucepan in the bowl of ice water and let stand, stirring once or twice, until thickened and cooled to room temperature, about 5 minutes.

4. Spoon half the chopped nuts into 4 sundae dishes. Spoon half the tapioca on top, then add another layer of nuts and another layer of tapioca, using both up. Cover with plastic wrap and refrigerate for at least 1 hour and up to 6 hours before serving.

5. When ready to serve, combine the remaining ½ cup of heavy cream and the remaining 2 tablespoons of granulated sugar in a small bowl and, using an electric mixer, whip until it just holds stiff peaks. Top each parfait with a dollop of whipped cream. Serve immediately.

Maple Mousse and Granola Parfaits *Serves 4*

I am a fiend for granola and love to think of new ways to use it. Here it becomes a wonderful foil for creamy maple mousse. I am partial to homemade granola with walnuts and dried cranberries, but you may use any kind, homemade or store-bought, that you like. I like to heat up a little bit of maple syrup to pour over the chilled parfaits just before serving, but that is optional.

4 large eggs

¾ cup pure maple syrup plus ¼ cup for drizzling, if desired

½ teaspoon maple extract

1¼ cups heavy cream, chilled

½ cup granola

1. Bring a small saucepan filled with 2 inches of water to a bare simmer. Combine the eggs and maple syrup in a stainless-steel bowl large enough to rest on top of the saucepan and set it over the pan, making sure it doesn't touch the water. Heat, whisking constantly, until slightly thickened and light in color, 6 to 8 minutes. Remove from the heat and, using an electric mixer, whip until completely cool, 7 to 10 minutes. Stir in the maple extract. Wash and dry the beaters.

2. In a medium-size bowl, using the mixer, whip the heavy cream until stiff peaks form. In three separate additions, gently fold the whipped cream into the maple mixture, being careful not to deflate the cream.

3. Spoon half the granola into 4 sundae dishes. Spoon half the maple mousse on top, then add another layer of granola and another layer of mousse, using both up. Cover with plastic wrap and refrigerate for at least 1 hour and up to 6 hours before serving.

4. If desired, heat the remaining ¼ cup of maple syrup in a small saucepan until warm, transfer to a small pitcher, and serve on the side with the parfaits.

Caramel Banana Pudding Parfaits *Serves 6*

Banana pudding made with vanilla wafer cookies is a time-honored icebox dessert. Most versions are made by layering cookies, bananas, and pastry cream in a baking dish, topping the whole thing with meringue, then browning it in the oven before refrigerating. I wanted to come up with something simpler. In place of pastry cream I use sweetened whipped cream, and I toss the bananas in caramel sauce to give the dessert some gooey richness. To crush the vanilla wafers, place them in a zipper-top bag, seal, and roll a rolling pin over the bag several times.

¾ cup plus 1 tablespoon sugar

¼ cup water

2 cups heavy cream, chilled

2 teaspoons vanilla extract

2 medium-size ripe bananas

20 vanilla wafers, coarsely crushed

1. Combine ¾ cup of the sugar and the water in a small heavy saucepan, bring to a boil, and let boil until it turns a light amber color. Do not stir. If part of the syrup is turning darker than the rest, gently tilt the pan to even out the cooking. When the syrup is a uniform amber color, stir in ½ cup of the heavy cream with a long-handled spoon. Be very careful, because it will bubble up. Transfer to a heatproof measuring cup, stir in 1 teaspoon of the vanilla, and let cool for 5 to 10 minutes.

2. Peel the bananas and, over a small bowl, cut into ¼-inch-thick rounds. Pour the syrup over them, toss gently to coat, and let cool completely.

3. In a medium-size bowl, using an electric mixer, whip together the remaining 1½ cups of cream, the remaining 1 tablespoon of sugar, and the remaining 1 teaspoon of vanilla until it just holds stiff peaks.

4. Sprinkle half the crushed cookies into 6 sundae dishes or parfait glasses. Spoon half the whipped cream on top. Spoon half the caramel-coated bananas on top of the whipped cream. Repeat so that you have two layers each of cookies, whipped cream, and bananas. Cover with plastic wrap and refrigerate for at least 1 hour and up to 3 hours before serving.

CHAPTER 4

Icebox Spectacular: Trifles and Charlottes

Whether it is a holiday dinner, baby shower luncheon, or graduation celebration, a grand occasion merits a grand finale. If you need a do-ahead dessert to feed a crowd, a dessert that is as spectacular to behold as it is to consume, then you've come to the right place. The layered extravaganzas in this chapter epitomize icebox ease. All can be made with store-bought pound cake, cookies, or bread. Most require little or no cooking. And the hours they need to set up in the refrigerator leave you free for other party preparations or just plain relaxation.

Generally speaking, a trifle is a giant parfait, constructed of layers of cake, pastry cream, fruit, and whipped cream. To my taste, pound cake is the best base for a fruit and cream trifle. Drier cake, such as sponge cake, and cookies are *too* dry, soaking up too much moisture from the fruit and cream and making the dessert less luxuriously wobbly. My recipes work with both homemade and store-bought all-butter pound cake (I use the Sara Lee brand). Because pound cake is so much moister than sponge cake or ladyfinger cookies, I figured I could skip the step of soaking the cake slices with sugar syrup and liqueur, but I found that trifles made that way were too dry.

Pastry cream or lemon curd supplies the creaminess essential to the dessert. Recipes for both are included here. They are not difficult, but they do require a watchful eye. The big danger is cooking them at too high a temperature, or for too long, either of which will result in a curdled cream.

The trifle is not a spur-of-the-moment dessert. Once it is put together, it should sit in the refrigerator for at least 3 hours and up to 1 day. This gives the flavors and ingredients a chance to meld. But do wait until the last minute to top your trifle with whipped cream.

The charlotte is a more tailored cousin of the trifle. Ladyfingers are arranged on the bottom and sides of a round, deep dish, then the dish is filled with mousse. Use American-style ladyfingers, which are softer and spongier than Italian *savoiardi*. The Italian imports are too dry and crisp for this type of treatment. I confess that I don't own a special charlotte mold and instead use an old soufflé dish for the task. When unmolded, the cookies create a pretty pattern and contain the filling long enough for you to display your creation to an admiring crowd. After the oohs and aahs, return to the kitchen and spoon it onto dessert plates. If there is a neat way to serve charlottes and trifles, I haven't discovered it, so I like to show them off *before* tragically ruining their good looks.

Pastry Cream *Makes 4 cups*

This is my basic pastry cream recipe, which can be used in tarts as well as trifles.

4 cups half-and-half

1 cup sugar

Pinch of salt

5 large eggs

5 tablespoons cornstarch

½ cup (1 stick) unsalted butter, cut into
  8 pieces

1 tablespoon vanilla extract

1. Combine the half-and-half, ¾ cup of the sugar, and the salt in a large heavy saucepan and bring to a simmer over medium heat, whisking frequently.

2. Meanwhile, in a large bowl, whisk together the eggs, cornstarch, and the remaining ¼ cup of sugar until pale yellow and smooth, about 1 minute.

3. When the half-and-half mixture is simmering, remove from the heat and gradually whisk it into the egg mixture, going slowly and whisking constantly so as not to curdle the eggs. Return the mixture to the pan and cook over medium heat, whisking constantly, just until a few bubbles break through the surface and the mixture has thickened and is shiny, 1 to 2 minutes.

4. Remove from the heat and whisk in the butter, one piece at a time, and the vanilla. Pour through a fine mesh strainer into a heatproof bowl and press plastic wrap directly onto the surface of the hot pastry cream to prevent a skin from forming. Refrigerate until well chilled, at least 3 hours and up to 2 days.

Lemon Curd *Makes about 2½ cups*

This is a tart, colorful alternative to pastry cream for use in trifles, in icebox cakes and pies, and as an accompaniment to fresh fruit and/or a slice of pound cake. If you want to experiment with other flavors, you can also use this recipe to make lime or orange curd (just replace the lemon zest and juice with either lime or orange zest and juice).

6 large eggs
1 cup sugar
1 teaspoon grated lemon zest
¾ cup fresh lemon juice
½ cup (1 stick) unsalted butter, cut into
    12 pieces

1. Whisk together the eggs, sugar, and lemon zest in a medium-size heavy saucepan until smooth. Add the lemon juice and the butter and cook over medium heat, whisking constantly, until thickened, 7 to 9 minutes. Do not allow to boil.

2. Pour through a fine mesh strainer into a heatproof bowl and press plastic wrap directly onto the surface of the hot curd to prevent a skin from forming. Refrigerate until cold and thick, at least 3 hours and up to 3 days before using.

 Simple Uses for Lemon Curd

Lemon curd is a pastry arts basic and can be employed in dozens of ways to create a huge variety of desserts. Here are some of the simplest and best:

- **Lemon Mousse**: Fold unsweetened whipped cream into lemon curd. Spoon into individual dessert goblets and refrigerate for up to 6 hours before serving.
- **Lemon Curd and Scones**: This is a traditional teatime treat in England. Purchase the scones at a bakery and reheat at home, or make them yourself.
- **Lemon Curd and Berry Shortcakes**: Use lemon curd in place of whipped cream to fill store-bought or homemade shortcakes.
- **Lemon Curd Sandwich Cookies**: Use lemon curd to sandwich together homemade or store-bought butter cookies. Sift some confectioners' sugar over the cookies just before serving.
- **Lemon Curd Ice Cream Sundaes**: Use lemon curd in place of whipped cream on top of vanilla ice cream. Top the lemon curd with some fresh raspberries and a sprinkling of toasted sliced almonds.

Lemon-Blueberry Trifle *Serves* 12

This is a terrific, easy, summer dessert for a crowd, especially if you make it ahead of time and use store-bought pound cake.

¼ cup water

¼ cup fresh lemon juice

½ cup plus 2 tablespoons sugar

4 pints fresh blueberries, picked over for stems

2½ cups heavy cream, chilled

1 recipe Lemon Curd (page 67)

One 10- to 12-ounce store-bought pound cake or homemade from your favorite recipe

1. Bring the water, lemon juice, and ¼ cup of the sugar to a boil in a small heavy saucepan, stirring occasionally to dissolve the sugar. Let cool.

2. In a food processor, process 2 pints of the blueberries and ¼ cup of the remaining sugar until smooth. Transfer to a bowl and stir in the remaining 2 pints of berries.

3. In a large bowl, using an electric mixer, whip 1½ cups of the heavy cream until it just holds stiff peaks. Gently fold in the lemon curd so you don't deflate the cream.

4. Cut the pound cake into 12 slices, arrange on a baking sheet, and brush each lightly with the sugar syrup. Cut each slice into 6 cubes. Tightly arrange one-third of the cubes in the bottom of a trifle bowl or large soufflé dish. Spread one-third of the lemon curd mixture on top of the cake cubes, smoothing with a rubber spatula. Spoon one-third of the blueberry mixture over the lemon curd. Repeat twice, so that you have three layers each of cake, lemon curd, and blueberries. Cover with plastic wrap and refrigerate for at least 3 hours and up to 1 day.

5. When ready to serve, in a small bowl, using an electric mixer, whip together the remaining 1 cup of heavy cream and the remaining 2 tablespoons of sugar until it just holds stiff peaks. Spread over the top of the trifle or use a pastry bag fitted with a large star tip to pipe it decoratively. Serve immediately.

Cranberry-Walnut Trifle *Serves* 12

Tart cranberries cut the richness and sweetness of this super-indulgent dessert, which is perfect for the fall and winter. A little rum in the soaking syrup adds holiday cheer.

1¼ cups water

¼ cup dark rum

½ cup granulated sugar

1 cup firmly packed light brown sugar

½ teaspoon ground cinnamon

½ teaspoon ground ginger

One 12-ounce bag fresh cranberries, picked over, with about 24 pretty cranberries reserved for garnish

1¼ cups walnuts, coarsely chopped

One 10- to 12-ounce store-bought pound cake or homemade from your favorite recipe

1 recipe Pastry Cream (page 66)

1½ cups heavy cream, chilled

1. Combine ¼ cup of the water, the rum, and ¼ cup of the granulated sugar in a small heavy saucepan and bring to a boil, stirring occasionally, until the sugar dissolves. Let cool to room temperature.

2. Combine the remaining 1 cup of water, the brown sugar, the cinnamon, the ginger, and the cranberries in a large heavy saucepan and bring to a boil. Reduce the heat to medium-low and simmer until the sugar is dissolved and the cranberries have begun to fall apart, 5 to 7 minutes. Remove from the heat, stir in 1 cup of the walnuts, and let cool completely.

3. Cut the pound cake into 12 slices, arrange on a baking sheet, and brush lightly with the sugar syrup. Cut each slice into 6 cubes. Tightly arrange one-third of the cubes in the bottom of a trifle bowl or large soufflé dish. Spread one-third of the pastry cream on top of the cake cubes, smoothing with a rubber spatula. Spread one-third of the cranberry mixture on top of the pastry cream. Repeat twice, so you have three layers each of cake, pastry cream, and cranberries. Cover with plastic wrap and refrigerate for at least 3 hours and up to 1 day.

4. When ready to serve, in a medium-size bowl, using an electric mixer, whip the heavy cream and the remaining ¼ cup of granulated sugar until it just holds stiff peaks. Spread over the top of the trifle or use a pastry bag fitted with a large star tip to pipe it decoratively. Top each rosette with a whole cranberry. Sprinkle with the remaining ¼ cup of chopped walnuts. Serve immediately.

Holiday Eggnog Trifle with Dried Figs and Hazelnuts *Serves 12*

Eggnog spices—cinnamon, nutmeg, and cloves—spike plain pastry cream in this grand holiday dessert. Look for very moist, soft figs—they combine wonderfully with the eggnog pastry cream and luxurious hazelnuts. If the figs you purchase turn out to be a little dry, place them in a heatproof bowl, pour over some boiling water, and let stand until plump, about 5 minutes. Drain and pat dry before using.

¼ cup water

¼ cup brandy or Cognac

½ cup sugar

1 recipe Pastry Cream (page 66)

½ teaspoon ground cinnamon

¼ teaspoon freshly grated nutmeg, plus extra for garnish (optional)

⅛ teaspoon ground cloves

One 10- to 12-ounce store-bought pound cake or homemade from your favorite recipe

24 dried figs (about 10 ounces), stemmed and coarsely chopped

1 cup hazelnuts, toasted, skinned (see headnote on page 39), and finely chopped

2 cups heavy cream, chilled

1. Bring the water, brandy, and ¼ cup of the sugar to a boil in a small heavy saucepan, stirring occasionally to dissolve the sugar. Let cool to room temperature.

2. In a medium-size bowl, whisk together the pastry cream, cinnamon, nutmeg, and cloves.

3. Cut the pound cake into 12 slices, arrange on a baking sheet, and brush lightly with the sugar syrup. Cut each slice into 6 cubes. Tightly arrange one-third of the cubes in the bottom of a trifle bowl or large soufflé dish. Spread one-third of the spiced pastry cream on top of the cake cubes, smoothing with a rubber spatula. Arrange one-third of the figs on top of the pastry cream and sprinkle with one-third of the hazelnuts. Repeat twice, so that you have three layers each of cake, pastry cream, figs, and hazelnuts. Cover with plastic wrap and refrigerate for at least 3 hours and up to 1 day.

4. When ready to serve, in a medium-size bowl, using an electric mixer, whip the heavy cream and the remaining ¼ cup of sugar until it just holds stiff peaks. Spread the whipped cream over the top of the trifle or use a pastry bag fitted with a large star tip to pipe it decoratively. Grate a little bit of nutmeg over the trifle, if desired. Serve immediately.

Beautiful Strawberry and Cream Trifle *Serves* 12

I love the combination of strawberry and orange, so I use orange marmalade and Grand Marnier in this trifle. Strawberry jam may be substituted for the marmalade, if desired.

¼ cup water

½ cup sugar

¼ cup Grand Marnier or other orange liqueur (optional)

4 pints fresh strawberries, hulled and cut in half

½ cup orange marmalade or strawberry jam

One 10- to 12-ounce store-bought pound cake or homemade from your favorite recipe

1 recipe Pastry Cream (see page 66)

1½ cups heavy cream, chilled

½ teaspoon vanilla extract

12 small fresh strawberries, hulled, for garnish

1. Bring the water, ¼ cup of the sugar, and the Grand Marnier, if using, to a boil in a small heavy saucepan, stirring occasionally to dissolve the sugar. Let cool.

2. In a large bowl, gently toss the strawberries with the orange marmalade to coat the berries.

3. Cut the pound cake into 12 slices, arrange on a baking sheet, and brush each lightly with the sugar syrup. Cut each slice into 6 cubes. Tightly arrange one-third of the cubes in the bottom of a trifle bowl or large soufflé dish. Spread one-third of the pastry cream on top of the cake cubes, smoothing with a rubber spatula. Arrange one-third of the marmalade-coated strawberries on top of the pastry cream. Repeat twice, so that you have three layers each of cake, pastry cream, and strawberries. Cover with plastic wrap and refrigerate for at least 3 hours and up to 1 day.

4. When ready to serve, in a medium-size bowl, using an electric mixer, whip the heavy cream, the remaining ¼ cup of sugar, and the vanilla until it just holds stiff peaks. Spread over the top of the trifle or use a pastry bag fitted with a large star tip to pipe it decoratively. Garnish with the whole strawberries and serve immediately.

Chocolate-Pear Trifle *Serves* 12

This trifle borrows its simple but perfectly balanced flavors from a favorite bistro dessert of pears with chocolate sauce and whipped cream. I was about to poach the pears for this dessert when it occurred to me that roasting them in the oven would be so much simpler. So sue me—this recipe does require a little oven time, but just to soften up the fruit before it goes into the icebox.

4 ripe pears, peeled, cored, and cut into
　¼-inch-thick slices

1 tablespoon unsalted butter, melted

1 cup water

¼ cup pear brandy or regular brandy

½ cup sugar

1 pound bittersweet chocolate, finely chopped

1 teaspoon vanilla extract

Pinch of salt

One 10- to 12-ounce store-bought pound
　cake or homemade from your favorite recipe

1 recipe Pastry Cream (page 66)

1½ cups heavy cream, chilled

1 tablespoon unsweetened cocoa powder

1. Preheat the oven to 400°F. Place the pear slices in a medium-size bowl, drizzle with the butter, and turn to coat. Arrange the slices in a single layer on a baking sheet and bake until soft and golden, 20 to 25 minutes. Let cool completely.

2. Bring ¼ cup of the water, the pear brandy, and ¼ cup of the sugar to a boil in a small heavy saucepan, stirring occasionally to dissolve the sugar. Let cool to room temperature.

3. Bring 2 inches of water in a medium-size saucepan to a bare simmer. Combine the chocolate and the remaining ¾ cup of water in a stainless-steel bowl big enough to rest on top of the saucepan and set it over the pan, making sure it doesn't touch the water. Heat, whisking occasionally, until completely melted and combined. Stir in the vanilla and salt. Let cool to room temperature.

4. Cut the pound cake into 12 slices, arrange on a baking sheet, and brush lightly with the sugar syrup. Cut each slice into 6 cubes. Tightly arrange one-third of the cubes in the bottom of a trifle bowl or large soufflé dish. Spread one-third of the pastry cream on top of the cake cubes, smoothing with a rubber spatula. Arrange one-third of the pear slices on top of the pastry cream. Drizzle one-third of the melted chocolate over the pears. Repeat twice, so that you have three layers each of cake, pastry cream, pears, and chocolate sauce. Cover with plastic wrap and refrigerate for at least 3 hours and up to 1 day.

5. When ready to serve, in a medium-size bowl, using an electric mixer, whip together the heavy cream and the remaining ¼ cup of sugar until it just holds stiff peaks. Spread the whipped cream over the top of the trifle, or use a pastry bag fitted with a large star tip to pipe it decoratively. Sift the cocoa over the top. Serve immediately.

Summer Pudding *Serves 8*

Buttery brioche adds richness to this summery, do-ahead dessert. If you can't find brioche, use a good quality artisanal country white bread. When cooked separately, the strawberries and blueberries maintain their distinct flavors and give the pudding a pretty blue-and-red-striped look.

2 pints fresh strawberries, hulled

¾ cup plus 2 tablespoons sugar

2 teaspoons fresh lemon juice

2 tablespoons framboise (raspberry liqueur)

2 pints fresh blueberries, picked over for stems

1 loaf brioche, crusts removed and cut into ⅓-inch-thick slices

1 cup heavy cream, chilled

2 tablespoons sour cream

1. Combine the strawberries and 6 tablespoons of the sugar in a medium-size heavy saucepan and cook over medium heat, stirring frequently, until the strawberries release their juices and begin to fall apart, about 10 minutes. Transfer to a bowl, stir in 1 teaspoon of lemon juice and 1 tablespoon of framboise, and set aside to cool.

2. Combine the blueberries and 6 tablespoons of the remaining sugar in a clean saucepan and cook over medium heat, stirring frequently, until the berries soften and begin to fall apart, about 10 minutes. Transfer to a bowl, stir in the remaining 1 teaspoon of lemon juice and the remaining 1 tablespoon of framboise, and set aside to cool.

3. Line a 9½ x 4 x 3-inch loaf pan with plastic wrap, making sure the wrap is tucked into all the corners and there is at least 1 inch overhanging the top of the pan on all sides. Spread about ¾ cup of the blueberry sauce across the bottom of the pan. Place slices of brioche over the sauce, trimming as necessary so the bread completely covers the fruit in one layer. Spoon ¾ cup of the strawberry sauce on top of the brioche. Continue to layer five or six times, until all the sauce has been used, ending with a layer of brioche. The pan should be very full, almost overflowing. Tightly cover with plastic wrap and place another loaf pan filled with dried beans or pie weights on top. Refrigerate for at least 6 hours or overnight.

4. When ready to serve, in a small bowl, combine the heavy cream, the sour cream, and the remaining 2 tablespoons of sugar and, using an electric mixer, whip until it just holds stiff peaks. Gently tug the plastic wrap that lines the pan to loosen the pudding. Place a large cutting board over the pan and turn it over. Gently tap to release. Peel the plastic wrap off and cut into 8 slices with a sharp knife. Place each slice on a dessert plate, garnish with whipped cream, and serve.

Tiramisu Charlotte *Serves* 12

For a big Italian dinner party, I decided to serve this pretty charlotte instead of my rather messy-looking tiramisu. The ingredients are the same, but the arrangement is a little more elegant. The ladyfingers are not soaked in espresso, as in true tiramisu, but arranged along the sides and on the bottom of a charlotte pan or soufflé dish. The mascarpone filling is flavored with espresso to give the dessert that coffee kick. This particular filling is very light and airy, so keep the charlotte in the mold until right before serving, and display it to your guests as soon as you unmold it, before the mousse has time to deflate.

24 to 26 store-bought American-style
   ladyfingers
1½ cups heavy cream, chilled
2 large egg whites
½ cup sugar
6 tablespoons cold water
¾ pound mascarpone, at room temperature
1 envelope unflavored gelatin
1 tablespoon Marsala wine or brandy
1 teaspoon instant espresso powder
5 ounces bittersweet chocolate, finely
   chopped
1 tablespoon unsweetened cocoa powder

1. Line the bottom of a 1-quart charlotte mold or soufflé dish with a circle of parchment paper. Arrange 10 to 12 of the ladyfingers on the bottom in two rows, trimming one long side of each cookie so that they fit snugly against each other when placed end to end; the rounded ends should fit up against the side of the dish. You may have to trim the sides of the cookies at the end of the rows so that they fit. The entire bottom of the pan should be covered. Line the side of the dish by placing the remaining ladyfingers, rounded side facing out, upright against the dish as close to one another as possible. If the ladyfingers extend above the top of the dish, trim them so they come just to the top. Reserve the trimmed pieces.

2. In a medium-size bowl, using an electric mixer, whip the cream until it just holds stiff peaks. Wash and dry the beaters.

3. Place the egg whites in another medium-size bowl. Combine the sugar and 3 tablespoons of the water in a small heavy saucepan and bring to a boil. When the sugar syrup is at a fast boil, turn the mixer on high and dribble the hot syrup down the side of the bowl with the egg whites in a thin, steady stream, mixing all the while. Decrease the speed to medium and continue to beat until the egg whites hold stiff peaks and the meringue is completely cool.

4. Place the mascarpone in a large bowl. Fill another small saucepan with 2 inches of water and bring to a bare simmer. In a small stainless-steel bowl that fits over the saucepan, sprinkle the gelatin over the remaining 3 tablespoons of water and let soften for 2 minutes. Set over the pan and heat, whisking constantly, just until the gelatin melts, 30 seconds to 1 minute. Whisk it into the mascarpone, working quickly so that no rubbery strands form. Whisk in the Marsala and espresso powder. Gently but thoroughly fold the meringue and whipped cream into the mascarpone mixture at the same time.

5. Scrape half the filling into the lined mold. Sprinkle half the chocolate over the filling. Scrape the remaining filling into the mold, smooth with a rubber spatula, and sprinkle the remaining chocolate on top. Top the charlotte with the reserved ladyfinger scraps so the filling is covered. It is not so important to arrange them in a decorative pattern, because this will be the bottom of the charlotte. Cover tightly with plastic wrap and refrigerate for at least 6 hours and up to 1 day.

6. To unmold, remove the plastic wrap and invert onto a serving platter. Shake the mold sharply to release. Sift the cocoa over the top of the charlotte and serve immediately.

Chestnut Mousse Charlotte with Chocolate-Orange Sauce *Serves* 12

One trick to making a special dessert while avoiding a lot of work is to showcase an unusual ingredient in a simple way. Chestnut puree and candied chestnuts, available at specialty food stores and many supermarkets around the holidays, are so novel and delicious that they impress with ease.

24 to 26 store-bought American-style
   ladyfingers

Chestnut Mousse

One 10-ounce (250g) can unsweetened
   chestnut puree

½ teaspoon vanilla extract

1½ cups heavy cream, chilled

1 envelope unflavored gelatin

3 tablespoons cold water

2 tablespoons sugar

Chocolate-Orange Sauce

6 ounces best-quality bittersweet chocolate,
   finely chopped

1 tablespoon unsalted butter

1 cup heavy cream

¼ cup Grand Marnier or other orange liqueur

Candied chestnuts for garnish

1. Line the bottom of a 1-quart charlotte mold or soufflé dish with a circle of parchment paper. Arrange 10 to 12 of the ladyfingers on the bottom in two rows, trimming one long side of each cookie so that they fit snugly against each other when placed end to end; the rounded ends should fit up against the side of the dish. You may have to trim the sides of the cookies at the end of the rows so that they fit. The entire bottom of the pan should be covered. Line the side of the dish by placing the remaining ladyfingers, rounded side facing out, upright against the dish as close to one another as possible. If the ladyfingers extend above the top of the dish, trim them so they come just to the top. Reserve the trimmed pieces.

2. To make the chestnut mousse, in a medium-size bowl, using an electric mixer, combine the chestnut puree and vanilla until softened and smooth. Slowly pour in ½ cup of the cream, beating until well combined. Wash and dry the beaters.

3. Bring 2 inches of water in a small saucepan to a bare simmer. In a small stainless-steel bowl that fits over the saucepan, sprinkle the gelatin over the cold water and let soften for 2 minutes. Set over the pan, whisking constantly just until the gelatin melts, 30 seconds to 1 minute. Whisk into the chestnut puree, working quickly so no rubbery strands form.

4. In a large bowl, whip together the remaining 1 cup of cream and the sugar until it holds stiff peaks. Fold the chestnut puree into the whipped cream, taking care not to deflate the cream, then scrape into the prepared charlotte mold, smoothing with a spatula. Top with the ladyfinger scraps. It is not so important to arrange them in a

**Chestnut Mousse Charlotte
with Chocolate-Orange Sauce**, *continued*

decorative pattern, because this will be the bottom of the charlotte. Cover tightly with plastic wrap and refrigerate for at least 6 hours and up to 1 day.

5. To make the sauce, place the chocolate and butter in a heatproof bowl. Bring the cream to a boil in a small heavy saucepan and pour over the chocolate. Cover with plastic wrap and let stand for 5 minutes, then whisk until smooth. Whisk in the Grand Marnier. The sauce may be refrigerated for up to 1 week; reheat it before serving.

6. To unmold, remove the plastic wrap and invert the charlotte onto a serving platter. Shake the mold sharply to release. Pour the warm sauce over the top so it drips down the sides. Arrange the candied chestnuts in a ring around the top of the charlotte and serve immediately.

Mango-Raspberry Charlotte *Serves* 12

After developing so many rich trifle and charlotte desserts, I started to crave something a little lighter. Here's a sunny summer charlotte that is so fresh tasting and airy that it seems to levitate out of the mold.

24 to 26 store-bought American-style ladyfingers

3 medium-size ripe mangoes, peeled and flesh cut off the pit

3 tablespoons granulated sugar, or more to taste

3 tablespoons fresh lemon juice

1 envelope unflavored gelatin

3 tablespoons cold water

1½ cups heavy cream, chilled

2 pints fresh raspberries

¼ cup confectioners' sugar, plus more for sifting

1. Line the bottom of a 1-quart charlotte mold or soufflé dish with a circle of parchment paper. Arrange the ladyfingers as described in step 1 on page 78.

2. Process the mango chunks in a food processor until smooth. Push the puree through a strainer to remove any strings. Scrape into a medium-size bowl and stir in the granulated sugar and 1 tablespoon of the lemon juice.

3. Bring 2 inches of water in a small saucepan to a bare simmer. Sprinkle the gelatin over the cold water in a small stainless-steel bowl that fits over the saucepan and let soften for 2 minutes. Set over the pan, whisking constantly just until the gelatin melts, 30 seconds to 1 minute. Whisk into the mango puree, working quickly so that no rubbery strands form.

4. In a large bowl, using an electric mixer, whip the cream until it holds stiff peaks. Fold in the mango puree and ½ pint of the raspberries, taking care not to deflate the cream. Scrape into the prepared charlotte mold, smoothing with a rubber spatula. Top with the ladyfinger scraps. It is not so important to arrange them in a decorative pattern, because this will be the bottom of the charlotte. Cover tightly with plastic wrap and refrigerate for at least 6 hours and up to 1 day.

5. Meanwhile, combine the remaining 1½ pints of raspberries, the confectioners' sugar, and the remaining 2 tablespoons of lemon juice in a food processor and process until smooth. Push through a fine mesh strainer to remove the seeds. Scrape into a bowl or airtight container, cover, and refrigerate until ready to use.

6. To unmold, remove the plastic wrap and invert the charlotte onto a serving platter. Shake the mold sharply to release. Sift the confectioners' sugar over the top. Spoon the raspberry sauce onto the platter, all around the charlotte, and serve immediately.

CHAPTER 5

IF I HAD KNOWN YOU WERE
COMING, I WOULD HAVE
REFRIGERATED A CAKE:

Ridiculously Easy Icebox Cakes

Probably the best compliment I received while developing recipes for this book was from my husband when I presented him with the Bûche de Noël that appears on page 95. "You are an evil genius!" he exclaimed, when I sliced the cake to reveal not a labor-intensive jellyroll, but a boxful of chocolate wafer cookies that I had stuck together with whipped cream and peppermint candy mousse.

It may not be evil, but there is something devilish about no-bake cakes. I found myself cackling delightedly as I brainstormed about how to use store-bought pound cake, chocolate wafer cookies, vanilla crème sandwich cookies, and yes, Drake's Devil Dogs to make the fun, tasty, and very good-looking icebox desserts that appear on the following pages. Icebox cakes, with all their tricks and short-cuts, may be guilty pleasures, but I'll take my pleasures where I can get them, thank you very much.

What would my former culinary school classmates say if they saw my recipe for a truly beautiful icebox cake whose four layers consist of Devil Dog snack cakes? I don't know, but I do know that my kids and their friends eat it up.

Let it not be said that going to culinary school had no influence on my work. Mocha Icebox "Meringue" Cake is an homage to one of my favorite class assignments, an elegant dessert made by spreading lightened pastry cream between two layers of crisp meringue. My version uses vanilla wafer sandwich cookies in place of the meringue layers and coffee-flavored pastry cream in the middle and on top.

If I were choosing on looks alone, I'd pick the two chocolate wafer cookie recipes in this chapter as my favorites. Pop Art Raspberry Icebox Cake uses the cookies for decoration and in place of cake layers. Cookies layered with super-simple, very pretty raspberry mousse give the cake structure and a nice striped look when sliced. Chocolate-dipped wafer cookies placed strategically on the bottom and sides of a plastic wrap–lined loaf pan become giant chocolate polka dots when the cake is removed from the pan. The Chocolate-Peppermint Bûche de Noël not only looks like the jelly-roll cake on which it is based, but, covered with cocoa whipped cream that has been striated with the tines of a fork to simulate bark, it also looks like an actual log, a trick that impressed my family no end. Don't forget the spearmint leaf candy garnish.

Peach-Almond Icebox Cupcakes *Makes 12 cupcakes*

Although these look like conventional cupcakes, they contain a delightful surprise: Under the almond-flavored whipped cream frosting hides a scoop of peach ice cream and a circle of rich pound cake—great for a late summer birthday party. Other flavors of ice cream and jam may be substituted, and chocolate pound cake may be used in place of the vanilla. Strawberry ice cream is very good with the almond whipped cream, as are chocolate and coffee. If you use strawberry ice cream, use strawberry jam in place of the peach and garnish the cupcakes with red sprinkles instead of toasted sliced almonds. If you use chocolate ice cream, try raspberry jam and chocolate sprinkles. With coffee ice cream, skip the jam but keep the nuts.

One 10- to 12-ounce store-bought pound
   cake or homemade from your favorite recipe
¼ cup peach preserves
2 pints peach ice cream
1½ cups heavy cream, chilled
⅓ cup confectioners' sugar
½ teaspoon almond extract
½ cup chopped almonds (optional), toasted
   in a 350°F oven until lightly browned, about
   8 minutes

1. Arrange 12 paper liners in a 12-cup muffin tin. Cut the pound cake into ½-inch-thick slices. Use a 2-inch biscuit cutter to cut 12 circles from the slices. Reserve the remaining pound cake and scraps for another use.

2. Spread 1 teaspoon of preserves on top of each pound cake circle. Place a circle in the bottom of each cupcake liner. Place a nicely rounded ⅓-cup scoop of ice cream on top of each pound cake circle. Cover the muffin tin with plastic wrap and place in the freezer until the ice cream is very firm, at least 2 hours and up to 2 days.

3. Combine the heavy cream, confectioners' sugar, and almond extract in a medium-size bowl and, using an electric mixer, whip until it holds stiff peaks.

4. Remove the muffin tin from the freezer and cover the ice cream with the whipped cream, leaving the cakes in the tin. Return to the freezer to allow the topping to set, at least 2 hours and up to 1 day.

5. Garnish with chopped, toasted almonds, if desired.

Coeurs à la Crème   *Serves 6*

I've always wanted to try this classic French dessert, and writing *Icebox Desserts* has given me the opportunity. Simply put, coeurs à la crème are little heart-shaped icebox cheesecakes. To make them, you just combine sweetened cream cheese, sour cream, and heavy cream and drain the mixture of excess water by spooning it into cheesecloth-lined perforated molds. The very creamy, slightly tart little cakes are perfect on Valentine's Day garnished with heart-shaped sliced strawberries. For coeurs with no lumps, it is important to soften the cream cheese before mixing it with the sour cream and heavy cream. Heart-shaped molds are available in cookware shops.

One 8-ounce package cream cheese, softened
6 tablespoons confectioners' sugar
1 cup sour cream (don't use reduced-fat)
½ cup heavy cream, chilled
½ teaspoon vanilla extract
1 teaspoon fresh lemon juice
1 pint fresh strawberries, hulled and sliced
2 tablespoons granulated sugar, or more to taste
1 tablespoon strawberry liqueur (optional)

1. Cut a large piece of cheesecloth into six 6-inch squares. Wet them with cold water and wring out each so it is damp but not dripping. Place a square inside each of 6 small coeurs à la crème molds, with the edges overhanging the top of the mold. Place the molds on a rimmed baking sheet.

2. Using an electric mixer, beat together the cream cheese and confectioners' sugar in a large bowl until fluffy. Beat in the sour cream, ½ cup at a time. Add the heavy cream, vanilla, and lemon juice and beat until smooth. Divide the mixture evenly among the molds. Cover with the overhanging cheesecloth. Refrigerate the molds on the baking sheet until the excess moisture has drained off, at least overnight and up to 2 days.

3. Twenty minutes before serving, remove the molds from the refrigerator. Peel away the cheesecloth that covers the top and overturn each one onto a dessert plate.

4. While the coeurs are standing, combine the strawberries, granulated sugar, and strawberry liqueur, if using, in a medium-size bowl. Stir several times to dissolve the sugar. Spoon some macerated berries around each coeur and serve immediately.

Devil Dog Icebox Cake *Serves 8*

Out of professional pride I usually avoid processed foods, even when developing recipes for quick desserts. But there are always exceptions. A while back, when I was sitting in my pediatrician's waiting room, I came across a recipe that used Suzy-Q chocolate and cream snack cakes to make an icebox dessert. When sliced, this dessert looked like a multilayer cake because of the stacks of chocolate and cream layered in the loaf pan. I've never had a Suzy-Q, but I am well acquainted with Drake's Devil Dogs, the equivalent in the part of the country where I grew up. These were my absolute favorite lunchbox treat as a kid, so I had to try to make something similar with them. My kids were amazed, and they immediately begged for a cake made from Twinkies. You're on your own with that one, but here is my Devil Dog creation.

10 Drake's Devil Dogs or other crème-filled devil's food cakes

1 pint cherry vanilla ice cream, softened

1½ cups heavy cream, chilled

¼ cup confectioners' sugar

½ teaspoon vanilla extract

1 ounce bittersweet or semisweet chocolate, melted and slightly cooled

Maraschino cherries for garnish

1. Line the bottom of a 9½ x 4 x 3-inch loaf pan with a rectangle of parchment paper.

2. Place five Devil Dogs width-wise in the bottom of the pan. Spread the ice cream in an even layer over the cakes. Place five cakes width-wise on top of the ice cream. Cover with plastic wrap and place in the freezer until the ice cream is very firm, at least 3 hours and up to 1 day.

3. When ready to continue, combine the heavy cream, confectioners' sugar, and vanilla in a medium-size bowl and, using an electric mixer, whip until it holds stiff peaks.

4. Remove the pan from the freezer. Run a sharp paring knife around the edge to loosen the cake. Place a serving platter over the pan and turn over. Gently tap to release. Peel the parchment from the cake. Smooth the whipped cream over the top and sides of the cake with an offset spatula. Lightly cover with plastic wrap. Return the platter to the freezer to allow the whipped cream to firm up, at least 3 hours and up to 1 day.

5. When ready to serve, remove from the freezer. Dip a fork into the melted chocolate and wave it over the cake to form decorative stripes. Garnish the top of the cake and the platter with maraschino cherries. Slice and serve.

Chocolate and Orange Icebox Bavarian Cake *Serves 10 to 12*

It was my privilege to work on a wonderful book, *Dessert University*, with former White House Pastry Chef Roland Mesnier. He has a repertoire of incredible cakes filled with airy Bavarian cream, and I wanted to adapt his Orange Bavarian Cake for this book. The cake must be put together in stages to allow the Bavarian cream to set up and the glaze to harden. Store-bought pound cake simplifies the process, and the cake can be made well in advance, making it perfect for a special occasion where you don't want to be distracted with last-minute dessert preparation.

One 10- to 12-ounce store-bought pound
  cake or homemade from your favorite recipe
1 envelope unflavored gelatin
¼ cup cold water
5 large egg yolks
½ cup plus 2 tablespoons sugar
2 cups half-and-half
Zest of 1 orange, removed in one thick strip
  with a vegetable peeler
1 or 2 drops orange food coloring
2 cups heavy cream, chilled
¼ cup Grand Marnier or other orange liqueur
12 ounces white chocolate
¼ cup vegetable oil
½ pint fresh raspberries

1. Line the bottom of a 10-inch cake pan with a circle of parchment paper. Cut the pound cake into ½-inch-thick slices.

2. Sprinkle the gelatin over the cold water in a small bowl and let soften. Whisk together the egg yolks and sugar in a large bowl. Fill another large bowl with ice water and set aside.

3. Bring the half-and-half and orange zest to a boil in a medium-size heavy saucepan. Pour the hot half-and-half into the yolk mixture in a slow stream, whisking constantly. Return the mixture to the pan and bring just to a boil. As soon as it begins to bubble, pour it through a fine mesh strainer into a heatproof bowl. Whisk in the gelatin mixture. Return the orange peel to the mixture. Set the bowl over the bowl of ice water and let cool, whisking occasionally until it is just beginning to thicken but is still liquid. Stir in a drop or two of orange food coloring so that the mixture is pale orange.

4. In a medium-size bowl, using an electric mixer, whip the heavy cream until it holds stiff peaks. Fold into the cooled Bavarian cream mixture.

5. Brush the cake slices with the Grand Marnier.

6. Pour the Bavarian mixture into the prepared cake pan, smoothing the top with a rubber spatula. Arrange the cake slices on top, trimming them where necessary so they cover the entire surface. Press down lightly on the cake so the sides of the slices are submerged in the Bavarian. Cover with plastic wrap and freeze until completely firm, at least 6 hours and up to 1 week.

7. Bring 2 inches of water in a medium-size saucepan to a bare simmer. Combine the chocolate and oil in a stainless-steel bowl big enough to rest on top of the saucepan and set it over the simmering water, making sure it doesn't touch the water. Heat, whisking occasionally, until the chocolate is completely melted.

8. Remove the cake from the freezer and run a sharp knife around the edge of the pan. Hold the bottom over a gas or electric burner for several seconds to loosen the cake from the pan. Place a serving platter over the pan and invert, gently shaking to release the cake. Peel away the parchment circle. Place strips of parchment paper underneath the cake and extending outward an inch or two. Pour the chocolate mixture over the cake so it covers the top and runs down the sides, using a small metal spatula to cover the cake completely. Let stand until the glaze is hardened and the cake thawed, about 2 hours. Remove the parchment strips with any excess chocolate glaze. Garnish with fresh raspberries and serve.

 ## Improvising an Ice Cream Cake

An ice cream cake doesn't have to be as high-concept as Devil Dog Icebox Cake or Peach-Almond Icebox Cupcakes. You don't even need a recipe to create one.

Pick up some frozen pound cake, heavy cream, and a pint or two of any ice cream that you like at the supermarket. Then choose your pan—I like either a loaf pan or a round springform pan. If using a loaf pan, line the bottom with a rectangle of parchment or wax paper. A springform pan needs no preparation.

Cut some pound cake into ½-inch-thick slices and arrange them in the bottom of the pan in a single layer, trimming so they cover the entire surface. Spread a 1½-inch-thick layer of softened ice cream over the cake and top with another layer of pound cake. If you like, you can spread some chocolate, caramel, or butterscotch sauce over the ice cream and/or sprinkle with nuts before topping with the second layer of cake. Cover with plastic wrap and freeze until very hard, at least 6 hours and up to 1 week. If using a loaf pan, turn the cake out of the pan and onto a serving platter and peel away the parchment. If using a springform pan, remove the side of the pan and place the cake on a serving platter. Frost with 1½ cups of heavy cream that's been whipped to stiff peaks with ¼ cup of confectioners' sugar and 1 teaspoon of vanilla extract, then return the cake to the freezer until the whipped cream has firmed up, at least 1 hour and up to 1 day.

Decorate by pressing chopped nuts, sprinkles, or grated chocolate onto the sides of the cake, or cover the top with chocolate shavings, and serve with additional chocolate, caramel, or butterscotch sauce on the side, if desired.

Pop Art Raspberry Icebox Cake *Serves 6*

Strategically placed wafer cookies look like large polka dots when this cake is unmolded. Then, when you slice it, you see the stripes. Make sure the cake is fully frozen before slicing for the cleanest look.

27 Nabisco Famous Chocolate Wafer Cookies

2 ounces bittersweet chocolate, melted and slightly cooled

1 envelope unflavored gelatin

3 tablespoons cold water

One 12-ounce bag frozen raspberries

¾ cup sugar

2 cups heavy cream, chilled

2 tablespoons framboise (raspberry liqueur)

1 teaspoon vanilla extract

1. Line a 9½ x 4 x 3-inch loaf pan with plastic wrap, making sure the wrap is tucked into all the corners and there is at least 1 inch overhanging the top of the pan on all sides. Working with one cookie at a time, spread the more rounded side of 9 of the wafer cookies with a thin layer of melted chocolate and place 3 of them, chocolate side down, on the bottom of the pan. Place another 3 cookies against each long side of the pan, chocolate-coated sides facing the pan. Place the pan in the freezer.

2. Sprinkle the gelatin over the cold water in a small bowl and let soften for 2 minutes.

3. Combine the raspberries and sugar in a medium-size heavy saucepan and cook over medium-low heat, stirring a few times, until the sugar dissolves and the mixture is warm to the touch. Stir in the gelatin mixture. Let cool to room temperature, stirring occasionally.

4. Combine the heavy cream, framboise, and vanilla in a large bowl and, using an electric mixer, whip until stiff peaks form. Gently fold in the cooled raspberry mixture, taking care not to deflate the cream.

5. Remove the pan from the freezer. Pour all but one-fourth of the mousse into the pan. Smooth the top with a rubber spatula. Insert the remaining 18 wafers into the mousse, arranging them vertically in three rows of six so they are lined up with the chocolate wafers on the sides of the pan. Spread the remaining mousse over the wafers and smooth with the spatula. The pan should be full to the top. Cover with plastic wrap and freeze until completely set, at least overnight and up to 1 week.

6. To unmold, gently tug the plastic wrap that lines the pan to loosen the cake. Place a serving platter over the pan and turn over. Gently tap to release. Carefully peel the plastic from the cake. Cut into slices and serve immediately.

Mocha Icebox "Meringue" Cake *Serves 8*

One of my favorite patisserie treats is a cake made of two layers of crisp meringue sandwiching a layer of pastry cream and covered in whipped cream. How could I modify this classic so that it would qualify as an icebox dessert? I'd have to find a substitute for the home-baked meringue. One day when I was strolling up and down the aisles of my supermarket, I spied a package of crème-filled vanilla wafer cookies, which are sweet and crisp just like meringue, and a lightbulb went off above my head. This version is filled and frosted with coffee-flavored pastry cream lightened with whipped cream. The "layers" are created by gluing together the cookies with a thin coat of melted chocolate. Don't worry if some of the pastry cream mixture oozes out from between the layers or onto the baking sheet when you are putting it together. Once the cake is fully frozen, you can neaten it up by trimming away any errant frosting with a paring knife before transferring it to a serving platter.

2 cups half-and-half

½ cup sugar

Pinch of salt

2 large eggs

1 large egg yolk

2½ tablespoons cornstarch

¼ cup (½ stick) unsalted butter, cut into 8 pieces

2 tablespoons instant espresso powder

1 tablespoon vanilla extract

42 crème-filled vanilla wafer cookies

6 ounces bittersweet chocolate

1 tablespoon vegetable oil

1½ cups heavy cream, chilled

2 tablespoons unsweetened cocoa powder

1. Bring the half-and-half, 6 tablespoons of the sugar, and the salt to a simmer in a large heavy saucepan over medium heat, whisking frequently.

2. Meanwhile, whisk together the eggs, egg yolk, cornstarch, and remaining 2 tablespoons of sugar in a large bowl until pale yellow and smooth, about 1 minute.

3. Slowly add the half-and-half mixture to the egg mixture in a thin stream, whisking constantly so as not to curdle the eggs. Return the mixture to the pan and cook over medium heat, whisking constantly, just until a few bubbles break through the surface and the mixture has thickened and is shiny, 1 to 2 minutes. Remove from the heat and whisk in the butter, espresso powder, and vanilla. Pour through a fine mesh strainer into a heatproof bowl and press plastic wrap directly onto the surface of the hot pastry cream to prevent a skin from forming. Refrigerate until well chilled, at least 3 hours and up to 2 days.

4. Line a rimmed baking sheet with parchment paper. On one half of the baking sheet, arrange 14 cookies close together in two rows so that they form an approximately 6½-inch square. Repeat with another 14 cookies on the other half of the baking sheet.

5. Bring 2 inches of water in a medium-size sauce-pan to a bare simmer. Combine the chocolate and oil in a stainless-steel bowl big enough to rest on top of the saucepan and set it over the pan, making sure it doesn't touch the water. Heat, whisking occasionally, until completely melted and combined. Use a small offset spatula to spread the chocolate in an even layer over the cookies. Place the baking sheet in the refrigerator to allow the chocolate to set.

6. In a medium-size bowl, using an electric mixer, whip the cream until it just holds stiff peaks. Gently fold it into the chilled coffee pastry cream.

7. Cut a 7-inch square out of a piece of cardboard. Cover the cutout with a piece of aluminum foil, tightly folding the edges of the foil under the cardboard. Place one of the chocolate-covered cookie layers on the cardboard, chocolate side down. Spread one-third of the pastry cream mixture over it and return it to the baking sheet. Place in the freezer for 20 minutes to firm up.

8. Place the second chocolate-covered cookie layer on top of the first layer, chocolate side up, spread with half of the remaining pastry cream mixture, and freeze for another 20 minutes.

9. Arrange the remaining 14 cookies on top of the pastry cream to form another cake layer. Cover the top and sides of the cake with the remaining pastry cream and smooth with an offset spatula. Lightly cover with plastic wrap and freeze until ready to serve, at least 6 hours and up to 1 week.

10. Just before serving, transfer the cake to a serving platter and sift the cocoa over the top.

The Non-Baker's Best Friend: Nabisco Famous Chocolate Wafer Cookies

Although I could have written this book without using Nabisco Famous Chocolate Wafer Cookies, I wouldn't have been able to include some of my favorite icebox desserts. In addition to the two in this chapter, check out the following recipes and you too will become a fan:

- **Peanut Butter Mousse Sandwiches** (page 46)
- **White Chocolate–Mint Mousse Sandwiches** (page 47)
- **Grasshopper Pie** (page 110)
- **Raspberry Sorbet Truffles** (page 136)

Chocolate-Peppermint Bûche de Noël *Serves 6 to 8*

Here's a fun retro Christmas dessert. Sugared gummi spearmint leaves make a great garnish. Save a slice for Santa.

20 round red-and-white-striped hard
    peppermint candies

10 ounces best-quality white chocolate,
    finely chopped

2½ cups heavy cream, chilled

¼ cup sour cream, at room temperature

One 9-ounce box Nabisco Famous Chocolate
    Wafer Cookies (about 38 cookies)

2 tablespoons sugar

2 tablespoons unsweetened cocoa powder,
    sifted

Candy spearmint leaves for garnish

1. Process the candies in a food processor until crushed but not powdery.

2. Bring 2 inches of water in a medium-size saucepan to a bare simmer. Combine the chocolate and ½ cup of the cream in a stainless-steel bowl big enough to rest on top of the saucepan and set it over the pan, making sure it doesn't touch the water. Heat, whisking occasionally, until completely melted and combined. Remove from the heat and whisk in the sour cream and crushed candy.

3. In a small bowl, using an electric mixer, whip 1 cup of the remaining heavy cream until it just holds stiff peaks. Gently fold into the chocolate mixture, taking care not to deflate the cream. Cover with plastic wrap and refrigerate until slightly firm, about 1 hour.

4. Spread 1 tablespoon of the chocolate-peppermint mousse onto each wafer. Begin stacking the wafers together and standing them on edge on a long serving platter to make a 14-inch log. Don't worry if some of the mousse drips down onto the platter. Cover the log tightly with 2 layers of plastic wrap and reshape it into a log with your hands. Place in the freezer until firm, at least 6 hours and up to 1 week.

5. When ready to continue, combine the remaining 1 cup of heavy cream, the sugar, and the cocoa in a medium-size bowl and whip with the mixer until it holds stiff peaks.

6. Remove the cake from the freezer. Trim a thin piece diagonally from one end of the "log" and discard. Trim a larger 2-inch-thick piece diagonally from the other end and set aside. Transfer the log to a serving platter. Spread all but ½ cup of the cocoa whipped cream evenly over the log and the ends. Attach the 2-inch piece about two-thirds of the way along the top side of the log, pressing lightly so it adheres. Cover with the remaining whipped cream (to look like a bump on the log). Drag the tines of a fork down the length of the log to simulate bark. Freeze for at least 3 and up to 6 hours. Just before serving, garnish the platter with candy spearmint leaves.

No-Bake Blueberry Cheesecake
with Brown Sugar Oatmeal Crumb Crust *Serves* 10

This is a foolproof cheesecake recipe, delicious as an ending to a summer barbecue. Rolled oats added to the graham cracker crumbs give the crust a wholesome taste and texture. Chunky raspberry sauce adds color and flavor, and it takes about a minute to prepare! This one is a trusted standby in my repertoire, and once you try it you will see why.

Filling

1 envelope unflavored gelatin

¼ cup cold water

12 ounces (1½ eight-ounce packages) cream cheese, softened

1 cup heavy cream

3 cups fresh blueberries, picked over

1 cup granulated sugar

1 tablespoon fresh lemon juice

1 Brown Sugar Oatmeal Crumb Crust, prepared through step 1 on page 108, pressed into the bottom and 1 inch up the side of a 9-inch springform pan

Raspberry Sauce

2 pints fresh raspberries, picked over

½ cup superfine sugar, or more to taste

1. To make the filling, sprinkle the gelatin over the cold water in a small stainless-steel bowl and let soften for 2 minutes. In a food processor, combine the cream cheese, heavy cream, blueberries, granulated sugar, and lemon juice and process until smooth.

2. Bring 2 inches of water in a small saucepan to a bare simmer. Place the bowl containing the gelatin over the pan and heat, whisking constantly, just until it melts, 30 seconds to 1 minute. With the food processor running, pour the gelatin through the feed tube into the blueberry mixture and process until smooth. Scrape into the prepared crust. Cover with plastic wrap and refrigerate until completely set, at least 6 hours and up to 1 day.

3. To make the sauce, combine the raspberries and superfine sugar in a medium-size bowl and stir, mashing about half the berries with the back of a spoon and leaving the remaining berries intact. Let stand, stirring occasionally, until the sugar is dissolved. (This will keep in the refrigerator for up to 6 hours. Bring to room temperature before serving.)

4. Release the cake from the pan. Slice and serve the cake with the sauce on the side.

Simplest Chocolate Cheesecake *Serves* 10

I love the tangy taste of cream cheese combined with bittersweet chocolate. The not-too-sweet filling is enhanced by the sugary, moist Oreo cookie crust. Garnish with a layer of fresh raspberries, if desired.

20 Oreo cookies (to yield about 1½ cups crumbs)

2½ tablespoons unsalted butter, melted and slightly cooled

⅛ teaspoon salt

½ teaspoon vanilla extract

1½ pounds bittersweet chocolate

2½ cups heavy cream, chilled

½ cup dark corn syrup

Two 8-ounce packages cream cheese, softened

1. Preheat the oven to 350°F.

2. Process the cookies in a food processor until finely ground. (Alternatively, crush them in a sealed zipper-top plastic bag with a rolling pin.) Combine the cookie crumbs, butter, salt, and vanilla in a medium-size bowl and stir until moistened. Press the mixture into the bottom of a 9-inch springform pan, packing it tightly with your fingertips so it is even and compacted. Bake until crisp, 6 to 8 minutes. Let cool completely. (The crust may be wrapped in plastic and frozen for up to 1 month.)

3. Bring 2 inches of water in a medium-size saucepan to a bare simmer. Combine the chocolate, ½ cup of the heavy cream, and the corn syrup in a stainless-steel bowl big enough to rest on top of the saucepan. Set it over the pan, making sure it doesn't touch the water. Heat, whisking occasionally, until completely melted and combined. Let cool slightly.

4. Using an electric mixer, in a large bowl beat together the cream cheese and chocolate mixture until smooth. Wash and dry the beaters.

5. In a medium-size bowl, whip the remaining 2 cups of heavy cream until it holds stiff peaks. Gently fold into the chocolate mixture, taking care not to deflate the cream, then scrape into the prepared crust, smoothing the top with a rubber spatula. Cover with plastic wrap and refrigerate until firm, at least 6 hours and up to 1 day.

CHAPTER 6

A Slice of Heaven: Icebox Pies and Tarts

In this chapter, I return to the subject of my previous book, where I first explored the possibility of making a delicious homemade pie without actually baking the filling. After making dozens of pies for that book, I find myself still hungry for new variations on this delightful theme.

So here are some brand-new recipes. The fillings range from creamy to chocolatey to nutty to fruity, satisfying individual tastes and cravings. But all the pies have several characteristics in common.

First, each has a cookie crumb crust, which is easy to make, takes just a few minutes to bake, and maintains its crisp texture even after hours of contact with juicy fresh strawberries or moist yogurt mousse. See page 105 for variations on the basic crumb crusts. If pressed for time, you can use a store-bought crumb crust and still wind up with a great dessert.

Each pie and tart included here needs time in the refrigerator to properly set up. It is especially important with these types of desserts to chill them adequately before serving. Your guests are unlikely to notice whether a trifle or parfait is a little bit runny, because those desserts are eaten out of bowls or glasses that will contain any messiness. Pies and tarts, on the other hand, should slice neatly for the prettiest presentation. You wouldn't pull a pumpkin pie out of the oven before it was fully cooked; by the same token, allow your icebox pie or tart enough time in the fridge before presenting it at the table.

A note on serving: Crumb crusts are sturdy and may stick to the bottom of your pie pan if you don't slice through them cleanly and pick them up carefully. I've developed a two-implement technique for transferring neat slices to dessert plates. First, I use a sharp paring knife to cut through the filling and, importantly, all the way through the crust. Then I insert a pointy-tipped metal cake server underneath the slice and lift it from the pan. The first slice may be tough to remove without losing some crust, but subsequent slices are a breeze if you first use the knife, then the cake server in the way I've described.

Fresh Berry and Pastry Cream Tart *Serves 8*

This version of the French patisserie classic has a graham cracker crust in place of the usual pastry crust. I'm biased, of course, but I think the crumb crust provides a nice, sturdy container for the cream and berries and resists getting soggy the way pastry does. Any combination of berries may be used. In the early summer, I like to use tiny local strawberries (the big berries from California are too big, I think) for a more down-home tart.

Graham Cracker Crust

11 whole graham crackers (to yield about
  1⅓ cups crumbs)
1 tablespoon sugar
⅛ teaspoon salt
5 tablespoons unsalted butter, melted

Filling

2 cups (½ recipe) Pastry Cream (page 66)
1 pint fresh blueberries, picked over
½ pint fresh raspberries, picked over
½ pint fresh blackberries, picked over
½ cup red currant jelly

1. To make the crust, preheat the oven to 350°F. Process the graham crackers into fine crumbs in a food processor, then add the sugar, salt, and melted butter and process until the crumbs are moistened. Press into the bottom of a 10-inch tart pan with a removable bottom and all the way up the side, packing it tightly with your fingertips so it is even and compacted. Bake the crust until crisp, 6 to 8 minutes. Let cool completely on a wire rack. (The crust can be wrapped in plastic and frozen for up to 1 month.)

2. To make the filling, use a small offset spatula to spread the pastry cream in an even layer across the bottom of the cooled tart shell.

3. Combine the berries in a large bowl and very gently stir to mix. Pour across the pastry cream, using your fingers to spread them evenly.

4. Bring the jelly to a boil in a small heavy saucepan. Lightly brush over the berries to give them some shine. Refrigerate, uncovered, for at least 30 minutes and up to 2 hours before serving.

Lime Cream and Mango Tart *Serves 8*

This is a wonderfully simple fruit tart, with the sweetness of the mango offset by the acidity of the lime and cream cheese filling. If mangoes are unavailable, sliced strawberries placed on top right before serving are also very nice.

3 tablespoons confectioners' sugar

½ cup full-fat (not low- or nonfat) sour cream

¼ teaspoon vanilla extract

One 8-ounce package cream cheese, softened

½ teaspoon finely grated lime zest

1 Graham Cracker Crust, prepared through
   step 1 on page 100

1 large ripe mango, peeled and flesh cut from
   the pit into ¼-inch dice

1. Whisk together the confectioners' sugar, sour cream, and vanilla in a small bowl. In a medium-size bowl, using an electric mixer, beat the cream cheese until smooth. Beat in the sour cream mixture and lime zest. Use a small offset spatula to spread the filling in an even layer across the bottom of the cooled tart shell. Lightly cover with plastic wrap and refrigerate until firm, at least 3 hours and up to 1 day.

2. Scatter the diced mango evenly over the filling. Serve immediately.

Espresso-Walnut Tartlets *Serves 4*

Espresso powder is one of my favorite flavor boosters. It instantly enlivens the flavor of so many ingredients, including the rich nut filling of these little tarts. I like the way these individual tarts look, but if you prefer, you can make one 8-inch tart rather than four 4-inch tarts. A little scoop of ice cream is essential—I like coffee best, but chocolate and vanilla are yummy, too.

Graham Cracker Crust

11 whole graham crackers (to yield about 1⅓ cups crumbs)

3 tablespoons unsalted butter, melted

2 teaspoons granulated sugar

Pinch of salt

Filling

10 tablespoons (1¼ sticks) unsalted butter

½ cup plus 2 tablespoons firmly packed dark brown sugar

½ cup light corn syrup

¼ cup heavy cream

2¼ cups walnut pieces

1 tablespoon instant espresso powder

Pinch of salt

1. To make the crust, preheat the oven to 350°F. Process the graham crackers into fine crumbs in a food processor, then add the melted butter, granulated sugar, and salt and process until all the crumbs are moistened. Press evenly into the bottoms of four 4-inch tartlet pans with removable bottoms, or one 8-inch tart pan with a removable bottom, and all the way up the side of the pan(s), packing it tightly with your fingertips so it is even and compacted. Bake until crisp, 5 to 7 minutes. Let cool completely on a wire rack. (The crusts can be wrapped in plastic and frozen for up to 1 month.)

2. To make the filling, combine the butter, brown sugar, and corn syrup in a medium-size heavy saucepan and bring to a boil, stirring frequently. Stir in the cream, walnuts, espresso powder, and salt and return to a boil. Reduce the heat to medium-low and cook at a simmer (not a boil), stirring occasionally, for 12 minutes.

3. Scrape the hot filling into the prepared tartlet shells. Let cool to room temperature. Cover with plastic wrap and refrigerate until completely set, at least 3 hours and up to 1 day, before serving.

Coconut Custard Black Bottom Tart *Serves 8*

Chocolate and coconut are layered in this tart: The crust contains some flaked coconut, then there is the "black bottom" layer of chocolate spread on top of it, then the creamy coconut filling, which is, in turn, covered with cocoa whipped cream. You can even garnish the tart with grated chocolate or toasted coconut if you want to add yet another layer. Be sure to stir the cream of coconut well before measuring it, because it separates in the can.

Coconut Graham Cracker Crust

11 whole graham crackers (to yield about 1⅓ cups crumbs)
¼ cup (½ stick) unsalted butter, melted
⅓ cup sweetened flaked coconut
1 teaspoon coconut extract (optional)
⅛ teaspoon salt

Black Bottom Layer

4 ounces bittersweet chocolate, finely chopped
1 tablespoon water

Coconut Cream Filling

2 cups half-and-half
1 cup canned cream of coconut, such as Coco Lopez, stirred well
2 large eggs
¼ cup cornstarch
⅛ teaspoon salt
½ teaspoon coconut extract

Cocoa Whipped Cream Topping

1 cup heavy cream, chilled
2 tablespoons sugar
2 tablespoons unsweetened cocoa powder

1. To make the crust, preheat the oven to 350°F. Process the graham crackers in a food processor until finely ground. Combine the crumbs, melted butter, flaked coconut, extract, if using, and salt in a medium-size bowl and stir until the crumbs are evenly moistened. Press into the bottom of a 9-inch pie plate and all the way up the side, packing it tightly with your fingertips so it is even and compacted. Bake until crisp, 6 to 8 minutes. Let cool completely on a wire rack. (The crust can be wrapped in plastic and frozen for up to 1 month.)

2. To make the black bottom layer, bring 2 inches of water to a bare simmer in a medium-size saucepan. Combine the chocolate and water in a stainless-steel bowl big enough to rest on top of the saucepan and set it over the pan, making sure it doesn't touch the water. Heat, whisking occasionally, until the chocolate is completely melted and combined. Spread the warm chocolate across the bottom of the cooled tart shell. Let harden slightly.

3. To make the coconut filling, bring the half-and-half and cream of coconut to a simmer in a large heavy saucepan over medium heat, whisking frequently.

4. Meanwhile, whisk together the eggs, cornstarch, and salt in a large bowl until pale yellow and smooth, about 1 minute.

5. When the half-and-half mixture is simmering, gradually whisk it into the egg mixture, going slowly and whisking constantly so as not to curdle the eggs. Return the mixture to the pan and cook over medium heat, whisking constantly, just until a few bubbles break through the surface and the mixture has thickened and is shiny, 1 to 2 minutes.

Remove from the heat and whisk in the coconut extract. Pour into the tart shell and, while hot, press plastic wrap directly onto the surface of the filling to prevent a skin from forming. Refrigerate until set, at least 6 hours and up to 1 day.

6. To make the topping, combine the heavy cream and sugar in a medium-size bowl. Sift the cocoa powder through a fine mesh strainer into the bowl, then, using an electric mixer, whip until it just holds stiff peaks. Slice the tart and top each slice with a dollop of the whipped cream. Serve immediately.

 ## Beyond Graham Cracker Crust

The Graham Cracker Crust is a classic, and I use it all the time for icebox pies and tarts. That said, I like to play around with the formula to tailor a crust to a particular filling, or just for a change of pace. For a Chocolate Wafer Cookie Crust, see the recipe for Grasshopper Pie (page 110); for Shortbread Crumb Crust, see No-Bake Fresh Strawberry Pie (page 112); for Coconut Graham Cracker Crust, see Coconut Custard Black Bottom Tart (opposite); and for Brown Sugar Oatmeal Crumb Crust, see Lavender Honey and Yogurt Pie (page 108). Below are a few of my other favorites when improvising icebox pies.

- **Graham Cracker and Nut Crust**: Use 11 whole graham crackers; ½ cup of unsalted nuts of your choice; ¼ cup (½ stick) of unsalted butter, melted; and 1 tablespoon of sugar. Chop the nuts along with the graham crackers in the food processor.
- **Gingersnap Crust**: Use 25 gingersnap cookies; 5 tablespoons of unsalted butter, melted; and ¼ teaspoon of ground cinnamon.
- **Vanilla Wafer Crust**: Use 50 vanilla wafers; 5 tablespoons of unsalted butter, melted; and 1 teaspoon of vanilla extract.
- **Amaretti Crust**: Use 4 whole graham crackers; 24 amaretti cookies; 5 tablespoons of unsalted butter, melted; and ½ teaspoon of almond extract.

Milk Chocolate Ganache and Caramel Tart *Serves 8*

This milk chocolate tart is very simple and truly satisfying. With its gooey layer of caramel on top, it's like a big candy bar.

Ganache Filling

10 ounces best-quality milk chocolate, finely chopped

1 cup heavy cream

1 teaspoon vanilla extract

2 tablespoons unsweetened cocoa powder

1 Graham Cracker Crust, prepared through step 1 on page 100

Caramel Topping

¾ cup sugar

¼ cup water

½ cup heavy cream

1 teaspoon vanilla extract

1. To make the ganache filling, place the chocolate in a large heatproof bowl. Bring the heavy cream just to a boil in a small saucepan over medium-low heat, pour into the bowl, and let stand for 5 minutes, then whisk until smooth. Whisk in the vanilla and cocoa powder. Pour the ganache through a fine mesh strainer into the cooled tart shell. Cover lightly with plastic wrap and refrigerate until well chilled, about 2 hours.

2. To make the caramel topping, bring the sugar and water to a boil in a small heavy saucepan and continue to boil until it turns a light amber color. Do not stir. If part of the syrup is turning darker than the rest, gently tilt the pan to even out the cooking. When the syrup is a uniform amber color, stir in the heavy cream with a long-handled spoon. Be careful, because it will bubble up. Transfer to a heatproof measuring cup, stir in the vanilla, and let cool until still pourable but not very hot, about 15 minutes.

3. Pour the caramel topping over the chilled ganache, spreading it in an even layer with a small offset spatula. Refrigerate until the caramel is firm, at least 3 hours and up to 1 day, before serving.

Lavender Honey and Yogurt Pie *Serves 8*

Lavender honey is especially fragrant and flavorful, but any other favorite honey is fine in this wholesome-tasting pie. I think fresh peaches sweetened with a little honey and cinnamon are the perfect accompaniment, but plums, berries, or any other fresh fruit of your choice may be substituted. Use organic, whole-milk yogurt if at all possible. The Stonyfield Farm brand is widely available at supermarkets and natural foods stores.

**Brown Sugar Oatmeal
Crumb Crust**

11 whole graham crackers (to yield about
    1⅓ cups crumbs)
5 tablespoons unsalted butter, melted
½ cup old-fashioned rolled oats (not quick-
    cooking)
3 tablespoons firmly packed light brown
    sugar
⅛ teaspoon salt

Filling

1 envelope unflavored gelatin
3 tablespoons cold water
1 cup whole-milk yogurt
½ cup lavender honey
1½ cups heavy cream, chilled

Topping

2 medium-size ripe peaches, peeled, pitted,
    and cut into ¼-inch-thick slices
2 tablespoons lavender honey
¼ teaspoon ground cinnamon

1. To make the crust, preheat the oven to 350°F. Process the graham crackers in a food processor until finely ground. Combine the crumbs, melted butter, oats, brown sugar, and salt in a medium-size bowl and stir until moistened. Press into the bottom of a 9-inch pie plate and all the way up the side, packing it tightly with your fingertips so it is even and compacted. Bake until crisp, 6 to 8 minutes. Let cool completely on a wire rack. (The crust can be wrapped in plastic and frozen for up to 1 month.)

2. To make the filling, sprinkle the gelatin over the cold water in a small stainless-steel bowl and let soften for 2 minutes. Whisk together the yogurt and honey in a medium-size bowl.

3. Bring 2 inches of water in a small saucepan to a bare simmer. Set the bowl containing the gelatin over the pan, making sure it doesn't touch the water, and heat, whisking constantly, just until it melts, 30 seconds to 1 minute. Whisk into the yogurt mixture until smooth.

4. In a large bowl, using an electric mixer, whip the heavy cream until it holds stiff peaks. Gently fold the yogurt mixture into the whipped cream, taking care not to deflate the cream. Scrape into the prepared pie shell, cover with plastic wrap, and refrigerate until completely set, at least 6 hours and up to 1 day.

5. To make the topping, when ready to serve, combine the peach slices, honey, and cinnamon in a medium-size bowl. Slice the pie into wedges and serve each slice with some peaches on the side.

Ice Cream Pies

I can't think of a simpler dessert than an ice cream pie. It is always appreciated, and people will think you worked harder than you did. Choose any of the crumb crusts used for the pies in this chapter (and see page 105 for other crumb crust recipes). Choose 2 pints of your favorite ice cream as a filling. Let the ice cream soften on the counter (but don't let it start to melt), spread it into the cooled crust, cover with plastic wrap, and freeze until ready to serve, at least 2 hours and up to 2 weeks. Don't forget the whipped cream, hot fudge, butterscotch sauce, nuts, maraschino cherries, and other toppings that are good on sundaes but better on pies. Here are a few combinations to get you started:

- Cherry vanilla ice cream in a Chocolate Wafer Cookie Crust (page 110) with hot fudge, whipped cream, and maraschino cherries on top

- Coffee ice cream in a Graham Cracker Crust (page 100) with hot fudge and Marshmallow Fluff on top
- Rum raisin ice cream in a Graham Cracker and Walnut Crust (page 105) with caramel sauce and rum-soaked raisins on top
- Dulce de leche ice cream in a Gingersnap Crust (page 105) with white chocolate sauce and chopped crystallized ginger on top
- Pistachio ice cream in a Graham Cracker and Pistachio Nut Crust (page 105) with whipped cream and hulled and sliced fresh strawberries macerated in sugar on top
- Chocolate ice cream (or, even better, Ben & Jerry's Brownie Batter ice cream) in a Graham Cracker Crust (page 100) with whipped cream and walnuts in syrup on top
- Mango sorbet in a Coconut Graham Cracker Crust (page 104) with fresh raspberries and whipped cream on top

Grasshopper Pie *Serves 8*

Traditional grasshopper pies are flavored with a combination of green crème de menthe and white crème de cacao, but I prefer to use all crème de menthe for a brighter green color and mintier flavor. Make sure your cream cheese is at room temperature to avoid lumps.

Chocolate Wafer Cookie Crust

30 Nabisco Famous Chocolate Wafer Cookies
   (to yield about 1⅓ cups crumbs)
⅛ teaspoon salt
5 tablespoons unsalted butter, melted

Filling

1 envelope unflavored gelatin
3 tablespoons cold water
4 ounces cream cheese (half of an 8-ounce
   package), at room temperature
1¼ cups heavy cream, chilled
½ cup confectioners' sugar
¼ cup crème de menthe
½ teaspoon mint extract
¾ cup miniature semisweet chocolate chips

Chocolate Sauce (optional)

8 ounces bittersweet chocolate, finely
   chopped
¼ cup water
1 tablespoon crème de menthe

1. To make the crust, preheat the oven to 350°F. Process the cookies and salt into fine crumbs in a food processor. Add the melted butter and process until the crumbs are moistened. Press into the bottom of a 9-inch pie plate and all the way up the side of the pan, packing it tightly with your fingertips so it is even and compacted. Bake until crisp, 6 to 8 minutes. Let cool completely on a wire rack. (The crust can be wrapped in plastic and frozen for up to 1 month.)

2. To make the filling, sprinkle the gelatin over the cold water in a small bowl to soften for 2 minutes. In the cleaned processor, combine the cream cheese, ¼ cup of the heavy cream, the confectioners' sugar, the crème de menthe, and the mint extract and process until smooth.

3. Bring 2 inches of water in a small saucepan to a bare simmer. Set the bowl containing the gelatin over the pan, making sure it doesn't touch the water, and heat, whisking constantly, just until it melts, 30 seconds to 1 minute. With the food processor running, pour the gelatin through the feed tube and process until smooth.

4. In a large bowl, using an electric mixer, whip the remaining 1 cup of heavy cream until it just holds stiff peaks. Fold in the cream cheese mixture and chocolate chips, taking care not to deflate the cream. Scrape into the cooled pie shell. Cover with plastic wrap and refrigerate until completely set, at least 6 hours and up to 1 day.

5. To make the sauce, if desired, bring 2 inches of water in a medium-size saucepan to a bare simmer. Combine the bittersweet chocolate and water in a stainless-steel bowl big enough to rest on top of the saucepan and set it over the pan, making sure it doesn't touch the water. Heat the chocolate, whisking occasionally, until completely melted. Stir in the crème de menthe. (The sauce will keep, tightly covered, in the refrigerator for up to 2 days.) Slice the pie and pour a little of the warm sauce over each slice.

No-Bake Fresh Strawberry Pie *Serves 8*

This is a simple and absolutely scrumptious alternative to conventional strawberry pie. Well chilled and refreshing, it is as perfect for summer entertaining as strawberry shortcake, but without the hassle of baking the cake. A warning: frozen strawberries won't work here—they are too watery (not to mention tasteless). And whipped cream is an essential finishing touch.

Shortbread Crumb Crust

20 pure butter Walkers Shortbread Cookies
  (to yield about 1½ cups crumbs)
Pinch of salt
2 tablespoons unsalted butter, melted

Filling

5 tablespoons cornstarch
¼ cup water
5 cups fresh strawberries, hulled and
  quartered
1 cup granulated sugar
1 teaspoon grated lemon zest
2 tablespoons fresh lemon juice
1 tablespoon unsalted butter

Topping

1 cup heavy cream, chilled
2 tablespoons confectioners' sugar
1 teaspoon vanilla extract

1. To make the crust, preheat the oven to 350°F. Process the shortbread cookies and salt together in a food processor until finely ground. Add the melted butter and process until the crumbs are evenly moistened. Press into the bottom of a 9-inch pie plate and all the way up the side of the pan, packing it tightly with your fingertips so it is even and compacted. Bake until crisp, 6 to 8 minutes. Let cool completely on a wire rack. (The crust can be wrapped in plastic and frozen for up to 1 month.)

2. To make the filling, combine the cornstarch and water in a small bowl and stir until smooth. Combine 3 cups of the strawberries, the granulated sugar, and the lemon zest in a medium-size heavy saucepan and bring to a boil, stirring occasionally. Stir in the cornstarch mixture and cook over medium heat, stirring constantly, until thickened. Continue to cook until it loses its starchy color and turns bright red, 3 minutes longer. Remove from the heat and stir in the lemon juice, butter, and remaining 2 cups of berries. Scrape into the cooled crust. Cover with plastic wrap and refrigerate until completely set, at least 6 hours and up to 1 day.

3. To make the topping, when ready to serve, combine the heavy cream, confectioners' sugar, and vanilla in a medium-size bowl. Using an electric mixer, whip until it just holds stiff peaks. Do not overwhip. Slice the pie and serve each slice with a dollop of whipped cream.

Triple Chocolate Pudding Pie *Serves 8*

Three kinds of chocolate give this pie an incredible chocolate flavor. The espresso whipped cream cuts the sweetness and adds a complementary coffee flavor. If you are a real chocolate fanatic, use Nabisco Famous Chocolate Wafer Cookies or chocolate graham crackers in place of the plain graham crackers in the crust.

4 large egg yolks

¼ cup cornstarch

1¼ cups granulated sugar

½ cup unsweetened cocoa powder

3½ cups half-and-half

3½ ounces bittersweet chocolate, finely chopped

3 ounces unsweetened chocolate, finely chopped

2 tablespoons unsalted butter

1 teaspoon vanilla extract

1 Graham Cracker Crust, prepared through step 1 on page 100

Espresso Whipped Cream

1 cup heavy cream, chilled

2 tablespoons confectioners' sugar

1½ teaspoons instant espresso powder

½ teaspoon vanilla extract

1. In a medium-size bowl, using an electric mixer, beat the egg yolks until thick and pale, about 4 minutes.

2. Combine the cornstarch, granulated sugar, and cocoa in a medium-size heavy saucepan. Add 1 cup of the half-and-half and whisk until smooth. Add the remaining 2½ cups of half-and-half and bring to a boil, whisking constantly. Whisk about one-third of the half-and-half mixture into the beaten egg yolks, then return the egg mixture to the saucepan. Cook over medium heat, whisking constantly, until it comes to a simmer, then let simmer, whisking constantly, for 1 minute. Remove from the heat and whisk in both chocolates and the butter until melted and smooth. Stir in the vanilla. Scrape into the cooled crust. Place plastic wrap directly onto the surface of the filling to keep a skin from forming and refrigerate until completely set, at least 6 hours and up to 1 day.

3. To make the whipped cream, when ready to serve, combine the heavy cream, confectioners' sugar, espresso powder, and vanilla in a medium-size bowl. Using an electric mixer, whip until it just holds stiff peaks. Slice the pie and top each slice with a dollop of the whipped cream. Serve immediately.

CHAPTER 7

THE SECRET INGREDIENT:
Icebox Desserts
Made with Gelatin

Sherry Panna Cotta

Cappuccino Panna Cotta

Honey and Sour Cream Panna Cotta

Lime-Coconut Panna Cotta

Cocoa Panna Cotta

Easy Blancmange with Apricot Compote

Berries in Minted Gelatin

Champagne Gelatins with Grapes

Raspberry-Peach Gelatins

Fresh Strawberry Gelatins

Grapefruit and Campari Gelatin Mold

Shirley Temple Gelatins

Ginger-Limeade Gelatin Squares

With apologies to the milk shake, dessert is something that should be eaten with a spoon or fork, not sipped through a straw. Thus, all my icebox desserts must attain at least a semisolid state to earn their name.

Some icebox desserts are thickened with gelatin. Your first response to this may be negative. Do you associate gelatin with the Jell-O your mother made you eat when you had a 24-hour virus? It is true that gelatin does not have the ethereal glamour of whipped cream or the golden richness of egg yolks, but it just may be the hardest working ingredient in the icebox dessert pantry. And, given some respect, it is capable of truly remarkable kitchen magic.

First, let's distinguish between gelatin, which is a flavorless, colorless thickening agent, and Jell-O, which is a mixture of gelatin, sugar, and artificial coloring and flavoring. I use the former, not the latter, in the recipes that follow. The amazing thing about gelatin is that it is completely invisible in icebox desserts, yet it gives these desserts their shape. Without gelatin, Cappuccino Panna Cotta would just be coffee-flavored cream, and Shirley Temple Gelatins would be, well, Shirley Temples.

To get your gelatin to perform these feats of transformation, you have to follow several important steps, because gelatin is highly sensitive to temperature. First, it must be softened and dissolved; sprinkle it over a small bowl of cool water and let it stand for a few minutes until the powder has turned into a bumpy, translucent gel. Next, the gelatin must be heated until it completely melts, either by placing the bowl over a pan of simmering water or by stirring it into a hot liquid. These steps, together, activate gelatin's thickening properties. If either is skipped, your dessert will not gel.

When stirring warmed gelatin into a room-temperature or cold liquid, be sure to whisk it in quickly and thoroughly. If the melted gelatin is not completely incorporated into the other ingredients before it begins to set up, it will form unappetizing, rubbery strands. All of this may sound complicated, but it's not. In fact, unlike cornstarch and egg yolks, which will produce lumpy messes if not carefully tended, gelatin is a relatively forgiving thickener. I myself have curdled dozens of pots of custard and produced countless batches of gloppy pudding. But I can count on one hand the times I have failed with gelatin.

Sherry Panna Cotta *Serves 6*

Subtle, refined, understated—if this is the type of dinner party you long to throw, this is the dessert you should serve. There's nothing flashy about panna cotta made with sherry, but people who appreciate the finer things in life will savor its smooth texture and distinctive flavor. Fresh fruit of your choice is just right as an accompaniment.

1 envelope unflavored gelatin

3 cups half-and-half

6 tablespoons sugar

¼ cup dry sherry

½ teaspoon finely grated lemon zest

3 cups blueberries, raspberries, sliced strawberries, sliced peaches, and/or sliced nectarines

1. Sprinkle the gelatin over ½ cup of the half-and-half in a small bowl and let soften for 2 minutes.

2. Combine the remaining 2½ cups of half-and-half, the sugar, and the sherry in a medium-size saucepan and bring to a boil. Remove from the heat and whisk in the gelatin mixture for 1 minute to dissolve. Stir in the lemon zest.

3. Divide the panna cotta among six 8-ounce ramekins or custard cups. Let cool slightly, then cover with plastic wrap and refrigerate until set, at least 6 hours or overnight.

4. To unmold, fill a small bowl with very hot tap water. Run a paring knife around each panna cotta to separate it from the ramekin while holding it in the water for 30 seconds. Place a dessert plate on top, invert, tap the bottom, and lift off the mold. Scatter some fruit around each panna cotta. Serve immediately.

 ## More Gelatin Desserts

The recipes in this chapter use gelatin as their primary thickening ingredient. There are other recipes sprinkled throughout this book that use gelatin along with other thickening agents for added structure and stability.

Once you have mastered the panna cotta, you might want to move on to one of the following:

- **Molded Peach-Raspberry Mousse** (page 36)

- **Frozen Piña Colada Mousse** (page 45)
- **Frozen Margarita Mousse** (page 42)
- **Lemon Gelatin Parfaits** (page 59)
- **Chocolate and Orange Icebox Bavarian Cake** (page 88)
- **Pop Art Raspberry Icebox Cake** (page 90)
- **Lavender Honey and Yogurt Pie** (page 108)
- **Grasshopper Pie** (page 110)

Cappuccino Panna Cotta *Serves 6*

This is a sweet substitute for after-dinner coffee. Garnish with chocolate shavings or serve with warm chocolate sauce, if desired.

3 cups half-and-half
⅓ cup freshly ground espresso roast coffee
   beans
¼ cup sugar
1 envelope unflavored gelatin
½ teaspoon vanilla extract

1. Heat 1½ cups of the half-and-half, the ground espresso, and the sugar together in a small heavy saucepan, whisking to dissolve the sugar. Bring just to a boil, remove from the heat, and let stand for 5 minutes. Strain through a coffee filter into a heatproof bowl.

2. Bring 2 inches of water in a medium-size saucepan to a bare simmer. Sprinkle the gelatin over the remaining 1½ cups of half-and-half in a medium-size stainless-steel bowl and let soften for 2 minutes. Set the bowl over the pan, without letting it touch the water, and add the strained coffee mixture. Whisk until the gelatin is completely dissolved, 2 to 3 minutes. Divide the panna cotta among six 8-ounce ramekins or custard cups. Let cool slightly, then cover with plastic wrap and refrigerate until set, at least 6 hours or overnight.

3. To unmold, fill a small bowl with very hot tap water. Run a paring knife around each panna cotta to separate it from the ramekin while holding it in the water for 30 seconds. Place a dessert plate on top, invert, tap the bottom, and lift off the mold. Serve immediately.

Honey and Sour Cream Panna Cotta *Serves 6*

I like to serve this slightly tart panna cotta with sliced fresh figs or apricots in season, but blackberries and peaches are also wonderful. Don't try to use nonfat sour cream here. The success of the dessert depends on the integrity of the ingredients, including *real* sour cream.

1 envelope unflavored gelatin

1½ cups heavy cream, chilled

½ cup honey, plus more for drizzling

1½ cups full-fat (not low- or nonfat) sour cream

3 cups fresh fruit of your choice (sliced figs, apricots, or peaches, or whole blackberries or red currants)

1. Sprinkle the gelatin over ½ cup of the heavy cream in a small bowl and let soften for 2 minutes.

2. Combine ½ cup of the remaining cream and the honey in a small heavy saucepan and heat until it just boils. Remove from the heat and whisk in the cream-and-gelatin mixture until the gelatin is completely dissolved. Whisk in the remaining ½ cup of heavy cream to cool the mixture slightly.

3. Place the sour cream in a medium-size bowl and whisk the heavy cream mixture into it. Divide among six 8-ounce ramekins or custard cups. Cover with plastic wrap and refrigerate until set, at least 6 hours or overnight.

4. To unmold, fill a small bowl with very hot tap water. Run a paring knife around each panna cotta to separate it from the ramekin while holding it in the water for 30 seconds. Place a dessert plate on top, invert, tap the bottom, and lift off the mold. Scatter some fruit around each panna cotta, then drizzle the fruit with some honey and serve immediately.

Lime-Coconut Panna Cotta *Serves 6*

Using cream of coconut in panna cotta is certainly straying a bit from the dessert's Italian roots, but it is a winning variation and especially refreshing after a meal of spicy Asian-inspired food. The diced mango brings some color to the plate, but it is optional. Alternatively, you might garnish each portion with a curl of lime zest removed from the lime with a vegetable peeler.

1 envelope unflavored gelatin

1½ cups half-and-half

One 15-ounce can cream of coconut, such as Coco Lopez brand, stirred well

3 tablespoons fresh lime juice

½ teaspoon grated lime zest

1 medium-size ripe mango (optional), peeled and flesh cut from the pit into ½-inch dice

1. Sprinkle the gelatin over ½ cup of the half-and-half in a small bowl and let soften for 2 minutes.

2. Combine the remaining 1 cup of half-and-half and the cream of coconut in a medium-size heavy saucepan and heat until it just boils. Remove from the heat and whisk in the gelatin mixture until completely dissolved. Whisk in the lime juice and zest. Divide among six 8-ounce ramekins or custard cups. Let cool slightly, then cover with plastic wrap and refrigerate until set, at least 6 hours or overnight.

3. To unmold, fill a small bowl with very hot tap water. Run a paring knife around each panna cotta to separate it from the ramekin while holding it in the water for 30 seconds. Place a dessert plate on top, invert, tap the bottom, and lift off the mold. Scatter some of the mango, if using, around each panna cotta and serve immediately.

Cocoa Panna Cotta *Serves 6*

I was amazed, going through my files, that in all my years of making chocolate desserts, and in all my years of making gelatin desserts, I had never attempted to combine the two. Chocolate panna cotta is a bit lighter on the palate than pudding or mousse, so it is a good choice when you want a light, cold chocolate dessert to serve after a summer meal. Be sure to sift the cocoa powder through a fine mesh strainer before beginning so that your panna cotta won't have any lumps.

1 envelope unflavored gelatin
3 cups half-and-half
6 tablespoons sugar
6 tablespoons unsweetened cocoa powder, sifted
½ teaspoon vanilla extract
½ pint fresh raspberries

1. Sprinkle the gelatin over ½ cup of the half-and-half in a small bowl and let soften for 2 minutes.

2. Whisk together the remaining 2½ cups of half-and-half, the sugar, and the cocoa in a medium-size heavy saucepan. Bring to a boil, whisking often. Remove from the heat and whisk in the gelatin mixture until dissolved and smooth, about 1 minute. Whisk in the vanilla. Divide among six 8-ounce ramekins or custard cups. Let cool slightly, then cover with plastic wrap and refrigerate until set, at least 6 hours or overnight.

3. To unmold, fill a small bowl with very hot tap water. Run a paring knife around each panna cotta to separate it from the ramekin while holding it in the water for 30 seconds. Place a dessert plate on top, invert, tap the bottom, and lift off the mold. Scatter a few raspberries around each panna cotta. Serve immediately.

Easy Blancmange with Apricot Compote *Serves 6*

Blancmange, a rich pudding traditionally thickened with ground almonds, dates back to medieval times. I love the combination of almond and apricot, but if you don't have time to make the compote, the blancmange is also very good on its own or with sliced fresh fruit.

Blancmange

1 envelope unflavored gelatin

2 cups whole milk

2 tablespoons (about 2 ounces) almond paste

½ cup sugar

¼ teaspoon almond extract

½ cup heavy cream, chilled

Apricot Compote

1 cup dried apricots, coarsely chopped

1½ cups water

2 tablespoons sugar

½ cinnamon stick

½ teaspoon vanilla extract

1. To make the blancmange, sprinkle the gelatin over ½ cup of the milk in a small bowl and let soften for 2 minutes.

2. Combine the remaining 1½ cups of milk, the almond paste, and the sugar in a medium-size heavy saucepan and heat, whisking constantly, until just boiling. Remove from the heat and whisk in the gelatin mixture until dissolved and smooth, about 1 minute. Stir in the almond extract. Pour through a fine mesh strainer into a medium-size heatproof bowl, pressing down on any solids to extract as much liquid as possible. Place the bowl over a larger bowl of ice water and let stand, whisking occasionally, until the mixture is completely cool and has just begun to thicken.

3. In a small bowl, using an electric mixer, whip the cream until it just holds stiff peaks. Gently fold into the almond mixture, taking care not to deflate the cream. Divide among six 8-ounce ramekins or custard cups. Cover with plastic wrap and refrigerate until set, at least 6 hours or overnight.

4. Meanwhile, to make the compote, combine the apricots, water, sugar, and cinnamon stick in a medium-size heavy saucepan and bring to a boil. Reduce the heat to medium-low and simmer until the fruit is soft but not falling apart, 10 to 15 minutes. Discard the cinnamon stick. Stir in the vanilla. Transfer the fruit and syrup to a bowl or container and let cool to room temperature, then refrigerate until serving time, up to 3 days.

5. To unmold the blancmanges, fill a small bowl with very hot tap water. Run a paring knife around each to separate it from the ramekin while holding it in the water for 30 seconds. Place a dessert plate on top, invert, tap the bottom, and lift off the mold. Spoon some of the chilled compote around each blancmange. Serve immediately.

Berries in Minted Gelatin   *Serves 4*

This is a pretty, elegant, and simple way to serve mixed berries.

½ cup sugar

1½ cups cold water

¼ cup coarsely chopped fresh mint leaves,
  plus fresh mint sprigs for garnish

2 cups assorted fresh blueberries, raspberries,
  and blackberries, picked over

1 envelope unflavored gelatin

1. Combine the sugar, 1 cup of the water, and the mint in a small heavy saucepan and bring to a boil. Reduce the heat to medium-low and simmer for 5 minutes. Pour through a fine mesh strainer into a heat-proof measuring cup. Let cool to room temperature. (This will keep, tightly covered, in the refrigerator for up to 2 days.)

2. Divide the berries among four 8-ounce ramekins.

3. In a small stainless-steel bowl, sprinkle the gelatin over the remaining ½ cup of water and let soften for 2 minutes. Bring 2 inches of water in a medium-size saucepan to a bare simmer. Set the bowl over the pan, without letting it touch the water, and whisk constantly until the gelatin is completely dissolved, 2 to 3 minutes. Quickly whisk the gelatin into the mint sugar syrup, then pour the syrup evenly over the berries. The syrup should come to the top of each ramekin. Let cool slightly, then cover with plastic wrap and refrigerate until set, at least 6 hours or overnight.

4. To unmold the gelatins, fill a small bowl with very hot tap water. Run a paring knife around each to separate it from the ramekin while holding it in the water for 30 seconds. Place a dessert plate on top, invert, tap the bottom, and lift off the mold. Garnish each plate with a mint sprig and serve immediately.

Champagne Gelatins with Grapes *Serves 6*

This is a lovely, light dessert, sophisticated yet so simple to make. It's not necessary to use the finest French Champagne here. Less expensive Italian Prosecco or Spanish cava is a good choice. Peeling the grapes may sound like a pain, but doing so makes the finished dessert smooth and refined. If you have an extra 15 minutes, try it.

1 envelope unflavored gelatin

3 cups champagne or other sparkling wine, chilled

¾ cup water

½ cup sugar

3 cups seedless red grapes, peeled

1. In a small bowl, sprinkle the gelatin over ½ cup of the champagne and let soften for 2 minutes.

2. Combine the water and sugar in a small heavy saucepan and bring to a boil. Remove from the heat and whisk in the gelatin mixture for 1 minute to dissolve any lumps. Pour into a medium-size heatproof bowl and gently stir in the remaining 2½ cups of champagne, taking care not to beat out the bubbles. Cover with plastic wrap and refrigerate until firm, at least 6 hours and up to 1 day.

3. When ready to serve, fold the peeled grapes into the gelatin until evenly distributed, then spoon into 6 goblets or champagne flutes and serve immediately.

Raspberry-Peach Gelatins *Serves 6*

These are as refreshing as a glass of iced raspberry tea on a hot day. Two cups of fresh raspberries may be substituted for the peaches if you'd like.

1 envelope unflavored gelatin

3 cups water

½ cup sugar

4 bags Raspberry Zinger tea or other raspberry-flavored tea

2 tablespoons fresh lemon juice

2 medium-size ripe peaches, peeled and flesh cut from the pit into 8 wedges each

1. In a small bowl, sprinkle the gelatin over ½ cup of the water and let soften for 2 minutes.

2. Combine the sugar and remaining 2½ cups of water in a small heavy saucepan and bring to a boil. Remove from the heat and whisk in the gelatin mixture for 1 minute to dissolve any lumps. Add the tea bags and let steep for 5 minutes.

3. Remove the tea bags and pour the mixture into a medium-size bowl. Stir in the lemon juice. Cover with plastic wrap and refrigerate until firm, at least 6 hours and up to 1 day.

4. When ready to serve, fold the peach slices into the gelatin until evenly distributed, then spoon into 6 goblets or sundae dishes. Serve immediately.

Fresh Strawberry Gelatins *Serves 4*

This recipe combines sweetened strawberry puree with gelatin for a fresh-tasting fruit dessert. The gelatin has a nice soft texture, more like a slushy frozen drink than Jell-O. Taste the berries before you begin. If your fruit is on the tart side, you may want to add a tablespoon or two more of sugar. Serve in martini glasses for a sophisticated presentation.

1 pint fresh strawberries
1 tablespoon fresh lemon juice
1 envelope unflavored gelatin
1½ cups cold water
½ cup plus 1 tablespoon sugar
½ cup heavy cream, chilled

1. Reserve 4 small, unblemished strawberries for garnish and refrigerate. Hull the remaining strawberries, place in a food processor, add the lemon juice, and process until smooth. Scrape into a medium-size bowl.

2. In a small bowl, sprinkle the gelatin over ½ cup of the water and let soften for 2 minutes. Combine ½ cup of the sugar and the remaining 1 cup of water in a small heavy saucepan and bring to a boil. Remove from the heat and whisk in the gelatin mixture for 1 minute to dissolve any lumps. Whisk into the strawberry puree, then divide among 4 martini glasses or goblets. Cover with plastic wrap and refrigerate for at least 6 hours and up to 1 day.

3. When ready to serve, hull the remaining 4 strawberries. In a medium-size bowl, using an electric mixer, beat together the heavy cream and the remaining 1 tablespoon of sugar until it holds stiff peaks. Top each glass of gelatin with a dollop of whipped cream and a strawberry and serve immediately.

Grapefruit and Campari Gelatin Mold *Serves 6*

One of my absolute favorite summer cocktails is a glass of grapefruit juice over ice with a splash of the Italian aperitif Campari. The flavors are sweet-tart and refreshing; the color—orange verging on crimson—is gorgeous. I thought it would make a terrific gelatin mold, and it did.

2 envelopes unflavored gelatin
4 cups fresh grapefruit juice
⅓ cup plus 1 tablespoon sugar
¼ cup Campari
Grapefruit wedges and fresh mint leaves
   for garnish
½ cup heavy cream, chilled

1. In a small bowl, sprinkle the gelatin over ½ cup of the grapefruit juice and let soften for 2 minutes.

2. Combine ⅓ cup of the sugar and the remaining 3½ cups of juice in a medium-size heavy saucepan and bring to a boil. Remove from the heat and whisk in the gelatin mixture for 1 minute to dissolve any lumps. Stir in the Campari, then pour into a 1-quart ring mold or bowl. Let cool slightly, then cover with plastic wrap and refrigerate until firm, at least 6 hours and up to 1 day.

3. When ready to serve, combine the heavy cream and remaining 1 tablespoon of sugar in a medium-size bowl and beat with an electric mixer until it holds stiff peaks. Fill another medium-size bowl with very hot tap water. Dip the mold into the water for 30 seconds. Place a small platter on top, invert, and shake the mold a little bit from side to side until the gelatin slides out. Scatter the grapefruit wedges and mint leaves around the gelatin. Fill the center of the mold with the whipped cream. Serve immediately.

Shirley Temple Gelatins *Serves 4*

To the delight of my children, I turned their favorite night-on-the-town cocktail into a wobbly dessert. This is a nice recipe to make for the kids when you're serving Champagne Gelatins with Grapes to the grown-ups.

2 envelopes unflavored gelatin

3½ cups ginger ale, chilled

5 tablespoons sugar

1 tablespoon grenadine syrup

½ cup heavy cream, chilled

4 maraschino cherries with stems for garnish

1. In a small bowl, sprinkle the gelatin over ½ cup of the ginger ale and let soften for 2 minutes.

2. In a small heavy saucepan, bring 1 cup of the remaining ginger ale and 4 tablespoons of the sugar to a boil, stirring until the sugar is dissolved. Remove from the heat and whisk in the gelatin mixture for 1 minute to dissolve any lumps. Transfer to a medium-size heatproof bowl and gently stir in the remaining 2 cups of ginger ale and the grenadine, taking care not to beat out the bubbles. Pour into 4 high-ball or parfait glasses, cover with plastic wrap, and refrigerate until set, at least 6 hours and up to 1 day.

3. When ready to serve, in a medium-size bowl, using an electric mixer, beat together the heavy cream and the remaining 1 tablespoon of sugar until it holds stiff peaks. Top each glass of gelatin with a dollop of whipped cream and a cherry and serve immediately.

Ginger-Limeade Gelatin Squares *Serves 4*

The green food coloring approximates the look of green Jell-O, but the flavor of these squares is fresh and natural, coming from freshly squeezed lime juice and grated fresh ginger. A refreshing low-calorie dessert, this is great after a spicy meal.

3 envelopes unflavored gelatin

3½ cups cold water

¾ cup sugar, plus extra for dipping the lime twists (optional)

1 tablespoon peeled and grated fresh ginger

1 cup fresh lime juice

1 drop green food coloring

4 lime twists (optional)

1. In a small bowl, sprinkle the gelatin over ¾ cup of the water and let soften for 2 minutes.

2. Combine the remaining 2¾ cups of water, the sugar, and the ginger in a medium-size heavy saucepan and bring to a boil. Reduce the heat to medium-low and simmer for 5 minutes, stirring a few times to dissolve the sugar. Remove from the heat and whisk in the gelatin mixture for 1 minute to dissolve any lumps. Stir in the lime juice and a drop of green food coloring. Pour through a fine mesh strainer into an 8-inch square baking pan. Let cool slightly, then cover with plastic wrap and refrigerate until firm, about 3 hours and up to 2 days.

3. To serve, cut the gelatin into 1-inch squares and place 8 squares into each of 4 dessert goblets or sundae dishes. Garnish with lime twists dipped into extra sugar, if desired, and serve.

CHAPTER 8

Fun with Ice Cream

Crunchy Peanut Butter Ice Cream
Sandwiches

Ice Cream Sundae Cones

Raspberry Sorbet Truffles

Ice Cream Bonbons

Pistachio Ice Cream and Cherry Parfaits

Coffee Ice Cream and Brandied Fig Parfaits

Rainbow Sorbet Bombe

Rose's Watermelon Ice Cream Bombe

Orange Polka Dot Ice Cream Terrine with
Blackberry Sauce

Stars and Stripes Ice Cream Terrine

Mocha Almond Fudge Sundae Terrine

Although I often use store-bought ice cream as a layering ingredient in icebox cakes and pies, I also enjoy using it on its own, shaping it into quick and easy desserts almost as if it were modeling clay. Slightly softened, ice cream can be pressed into demitasse cups, ice cream pop molds, loaf pans, and bowls.

Developing the recipes in this chapter was like designing the curriculum for a preschool art class. Which colors of ice cream and sorbet would taste great together and also give me the brightest stripes when I alternated them in a loaf pan? How could I achieve a polka-dot effect with vanilla ice cream and orange sorbet? Because there's very little cooking involved in any of these projects, there's plenty of time to arrange the various flavors of ice cream and their garnishes so that they make an amusing presentation.

The trickiest thing about making any of these desserts is letting the ice cream soften sufficiently so that it is easy to work with, but not so much that it begins to melt. I have found that 5 to 15 minutes of sitting on the counter is necessary before the ice cream is ready. Check it every 5 minutes by inserting a knife into the center of the container and wiggling it to see whether the center is soft enough to scoop. Occasionally, a pint of ice cream just purchased from a very cold freezer at a convenience store is so cold and hard that its center will not thaw before the outer portion begins to melt. When this is the case, I pop it into the microwave oven for just a few seconds to thaw the inside core slightly.

Crunchy Peanut Butter Ice Cream Sandwiches
Makes 8 ice cream sandwiches

I had seen several versions of this ice cream sandwich recipe over the years, but I was never tempted to try one until I had kids, and their many cereal boxes began crowding my pantry shelves. Corn flakes also work very nicely here. My older daughter insists that chocolate-flavored rice cereal would be good, but I have not yet broken down and bought her a box to test her theory.

½ cup light corn syrup
½ cup smooth peanut butter
3 cups Post Grape-Nuts cereal
1 pint vanilla ice cream
1 pint chocolate ice cream

1. Line an 8-inch square baking pan with heavy-duty aluminum foil, making sure the foil is tucked into all the corners and there is at least 1 inch overhanging the top of the pan on all sides.

2. Stir together the corn syrup and peanut butter in a large bowl until well combined. Stir in the Grape-Nuts until all of the cereal is moistened but not completely crushed. Spread half the cereal mixture over the bottom of the prepared pan and press it into a thin, even layer with your fingertips. Place in the freezer for 15 minutes.

3. Set the vanilla ice cream out on the counter to soften for 5 minutes, then spoon in tablespoonfuls across the cereal layer. Use an offset spatula to smooth it into an even layer. Place in the freezer for 20 minutes to firm up.

4. Set the chocolate ice cream out on the counter to soften for 5 minutes, then smooth over the vanilla ice cream and place in the freezer for another 20 minutes to firm up.

5. Spread the remaining half of the cereal mixture over the top of the chocolate ice cream and press it into a thin, even layer with your fingertips. Freeze until very firm, at least 6 hours and up to 1 day.

6. Grasping the overhanging foil on either side of the pan, lift out the layers and place on a cutting board. Cut into 8 bars. Serve immediately.

Ice Cream Sundae Cones *Makes 8 ice cream cones*

Ice cream cones dipped in chocolate, rolled in sprinkles, and topped with a maraschino cherry are a fun do-ahead substitute for sundaes in dishes. A little vegetable oil keeps the chocolate coating shiny. Stand the cones upright inside juice glasses and keep in the freezer for up to 1 day before serving. Mix and match ice cream flavors with dark or white chocolate coating. Chopped nuts may be substituted for the sprinkles, if you like.

8 sugar cones
1 pint plus ½ cup ice cream
12 ounces semisweet chocolate, finely
   chopped
2½ tablespoons vegetable oil
¼ cup multicolored sprinkles
8 maraschino cherries with stems

1. One at a time, carefully fill the tip of each cone with about 1 table-spoon of ice cream and top with a ¼-cup scoop of ice cream. Press down gently on the ice cream with the back of the scoop to make sure that it is secure in the cone. Place each filled cone upright in a small juice glass, put the juice glasses on a baking sheet, and put in the freezer until the ice cream is very firm, at least 1 hour and up to 3 hours.

2. Bring 2 inches of water in a medium-size saucepan to a bare simmer. Combine the chocolate and oil in a stainless-steel bowl big enough to rest on top of the saucepan. Set it over the pan, making sure it doesn't touch the water. Heat, whisking occasionally, until the chocolate is completely melted. Remove from the heat and let cool to just lukewarm.

3. Place the sprinkles in a small bowl. Remove one of the cones from the freezer and, working over the bowl of chocolate, spoon some chocolate over the ice cream, coating it completely and letting any excess drip back into the bowl of chocolate. Hold the cone over the bowl of sprinkles and lightly cover the chocolate with sprinkles. Dip the bottom of one cherry into the chocolate and press it on top of the sprinkles. Return the cone to the juice glass and return it to the freezer. Repeat with the remaining cones. Freeze for at least 1 hour and up to 6 hours before serving.

Raspberry Sorbet Truffles *Serves 8*

These little bonbons are based on the famous Italian *tartufo*, served at outdoor cafés in Rome's Piazza Navona. Traditionally, a small scoop of chocolate ice cream encloses a brandied cherry center. Here, I've replaced the cherry with a smaller scoop of raspberry sorbet. The ice cream balls can be frozen for up to 2 weeks. Pour the warm chocolate sauce over them just before serving, so that it is still semisoft when the dessert is brought to the table. Don't skip the chocolate cookie crumbs, as they keep the bonbons in place on the plate. Without the crumbs, the bonbons will slide and possibly fly across the room on contact with a spoon!

2 pints chocolate ice cream, slightly softened
1 pint raspberry sorbet, slightly softened
7 ounces bittersweet chocolate, finely chopped
¾ cup heavy cream
1 tablespoon framboise (raspberry liqueur)
½ cup Nabisco Famous Chocolate Wafer Cookie crumbs
Fresh raspberries for garnish

1. Line eight ½-cup demitasse cups with plastic wrap so at least 1 inch of the plastic overhangs the edge of each cup.

2. Fill each cup with the chocolate ice cream and smooth the top with a small spatula. Use a very small ice cream scoop or melon baller to remove a scoop of the chocolate ice cream. Fill the hole with a small scoop of the raspberry sorbet. Cover each cup with plastic wrap and freeze until very firm, at least 4 hours and up to 2 weeks.

3. Place the chocolate in a heatproof bowl. Bring the cream to a near boil in a small heavy saucepan, pour over the chocolate, and whisk until smooth. Stir in the framboise. Let cool to lukewarm.

4. Remove the ice cream balls from the freezer. Place the cookie crumbs in a shallow bowl. Pull the ice cream balls from the cups and remove the plastic wrap. Dip the flat bottom of each ice cream ball into the crumbs and place, crumb side down, on a dessert dish. Spoon some of the chocolate sauce over each portion of ice cream so the sauce covers the ice cream and drips a little bit beyond. Scatter some raspberries around each plate. Serve immediately.

Ice Cream Bonbons *Makes about 20 bonbons*

Small scoops of chocolate ice cream can easily be made to look like bonbons by dipping them into chocolate. Roll some in nuts or flaked sweetened coconut, if desired.

1 pint chocolate ice cream

8 ounces bittersweet chocolate

1 tablespoon plus 1 teaspoon vegetable oil

2 tablespoons finely chopped nuts (optional)

2 tablespoons sweetened flaked coconut (optional)

1. Line a rimmed baking sheet with parchment or wax paper. Place the sheet in the freezer for 15 minutes to chill.

2. Use a 1½-tablespoon ice cream scoop to make balls of ice cream and place them on the chilled baking sheet. If the ice cream is getting too soft as you work, return it to the freezer, along with the scoops on the baking sheet, for 15 minutes to firm up before continuing. Lightly cover the baking sheet with plastic wrap and chill until very firm, at least 1 hour and up to 1 day.

3. Bring 2 inches of water in a medium-size saucepan to a bare simmer. Combine the chocolate and oil in a stainless-steel bowl big enough to rest on top of the saucepan and set it over the pan, making sure it doesn't touch the water. Heat, whisking occasionally, until the chocolate is completely melted. Remove from the heat and let cool to room temperature.

4. Remove the ice cream balls from the freezer and, working quickly with a fork in each hand, quickly roll a ball in the chocolate to cover. Pick up the ball by sliding it onto one of the forks, let any excess chocolate drip back into the bowl, and transfer the bonbon to the baking sheet. Sprinkle some with nuts and some with coconut, if desired. Repeat with the remaining ice cream balls. If the ice cream balls begin to melt while you are working, return them to the freezer for 15 minutes to firm up before proceeding. Freeze the bonbons until firm, at least 1 hour and up to 1 day, before serving.

Pistachio Ice Cream and Cherry Parfaits *Serves 4*

Pistachios and cherries are an all-time favorite combination of mine. Here, I serve them together in an ice cream parfait.

2 cups fresh cherries (about ¾ pound), pitted and coarsely chopped

½ cup granulated sugar

2 tablespoons kirsch or other cherry brandy

1 pint pistachio ice cream

¼ cup shelled, unsalted pistachio nuts, coarsely chopped

½ cup heavy cream, chilled

2 teaspoons confectioners' sugar

4 fresh cherries with stems for garnish

1. Combine 2 cups of the cherries and the granulated sugar in a medium-size heavy saucepan and bring to boil. Reduce the heat to medium-low and simmer until almost all the liquid has evaporated, about 10 minutes. Remove from the heat and stir in the kirsch. Transfer to an airtight container, let cool, and refrigerate until well chilled, at least 3 hours and up to 1 week.

2. Let the ice cream soften on the counter for 5 minutes. Spoon about 1 tablespoon of the cherry sauce into each of 4 parfait glasses. Place a small scoop of ice cream (about 2 tablespoons) in each glass and sprinkle with ½ tablespoon of the chopped pistachios. Repeat the layering one more time. Cover each glass with plastic wrap and place in the freezer for at least 1 hour and up to 24 hours.

3. Remove the parfaits from the freezer and let stand for 5 minutes. Place the heavy cream and confectioners' sugar in a small bowl and, using an electric mixer, beat until it just holds stiff peaks. Top each parfait with some of the whipped cream, then a cherry, and serve.

Ice Cream Parfaits

Some of the simplest and most delicious parfaits begin with a pint of store-bought ice cream. Here are some ideas to get you started, but do try some combinations of your own. Don't forget to top with sweetened whipped cream before serving.

- Dulce de leche ice cream, rum-soaked apricots, and sliced almonds
- Vanilla ice cream, brandied prunes, and walnuts

- Coconut sorbet, caramel sauce, diced fresh pineapple, and macadamia nuts
- Strawberry ice cream, white chocolate sauce, sliced fresh strawberries, and hazelnuts
- Mint chocolate chip ice cream and a chunky raspberry sauce made with a shot of framboise

Coffee Ice Cream and Brandied Fig Parfaits *Serves* 4

This is one of the simplest ways to enjoy the fantastic combination of coffee and figs.
For a simple variation, substitute rum for the brandy, dark raisins for the figs, and vanilla ice cream
for the coffee ice cream.

¼ cup brandy

6 dried figs, stemmed and coarsely chopped

1 pint coffee ice cream

¼ cup almonds, finely chopped

½ cup heavy cream

2 teaspoons confectioners' sugar

4 whole almonds for garnish

1. Combine the brandy and figs in a small heavy saucepan and bring to a simmer. Let stand until cool.

2. Let the ice cream soften on the counter for 5 minutes. Spoon about 1 tablespoon of the brandy-and-fig mixture into each of 4 parfait glasses. Place a small scoop of ice cream (about 2 tablespoons) in each glass and sprinkle with ½ tablespoon of the chopped almonds. Repeat the layering one more time. Cover with plastic wrap and place in the freezer for at least 1 hour and up to 1 day.

3. Remove the parfaits from the freezer and let stand for 5 minutes. Place the heavy cream and confectioners' sugar in a small bowl and, using an electric mixer, beat until it just holds stiff peaks. Top each parfait with whipped cream and a whole almond and serve.

Rainbow Sorbet Bombe *Serves 6 to 8*

A majority of the colors of the rainbow—red, orange, yellow, and green—are represented in this sorbet bombe, separated by crispy-creamy layers of crushed vanilla crème cookies. If you can find blue- and violet-shaded sorbet, by all means add them to the spectrum.

One 8-ounce package vanilla crème wafer
  cookies
1 pint raspberry sorbet
1 pint mango sorbet
1 pint lemon sorbet
1 pint lime sorbet
1 cup heavy cream, chilled
2 tablespoons confectioners' sugar
½ teaspoon vanilla extract

1. Line a 2-quart bowl with plastic wrap so it overhangs the side by at least 1 inch. Process the cookies in a food processor until crushed.

2. Let the raspberry sorbet soften for 5 minutes on the counter. Spoon the sorbet into the bowl, pressing it into the bottom and up the side with the back of a spoon to form a smooth layer. Sprinkle one-fourth of the cookie crumbs in an even layer over the sorbet. Place in the freezer for 20 minutes to firm up.

3. Let the mango sorbet soften for 5 minutes on the counter. Use a small offset spatula to smooth it over the raspberry sorbet in an even layer. Sprinkle one-third of the remaining cookie crumbs evenly over the mango sorbet. Place in the freezer for 20 minutes more to firm up.

4. Let the lemon sorbet soften for 5 minutes on the counter. Use the spatula to smooth it over the mango sorbet in an even layer. Sprinkle half of the remaining cookie crumbs evenly over the lemon sorbet. Place in the freezer for another 20 minutes to firm up.

5. Spoon the lime sorbet into the bowl so it fills the remaining space and comes to the top of the bowl. Smooth the top and sprinkle with the remaining cookie crumbs. Cover with plastic wrap and freeze for at least 6 hours or up to 1 week.

6. When ready to serve, combine the heavy cream, confectioners' sugar, and vanilla in a medium-size bowl and, using an electric mixer, beat until it just holds stiff peaks. Take the sorbet bombe from the freezer and remove the plastic from the top of the bowl. Gently tug at the overhanging plastic lining the bowl to loosen the sorbet. Place a serving platter over the bowl, invert, and shake to release. Peel away the plastic. Cover the bombe with the whipped cream, using a small offset spatula. Return to the freezer to allow the cream to firm up, at least 1 hour and up to 6 hours. Cut into wedges and serve immediately.

Rose's Watermelon Ice Cream Bombe *Serves 6 to 8*

Like so many of my children's favorite recipes, this one was inspired by something we saw while watching a television show. The kids on the show demonstrated how to make an ice cream cake that, when sliced, looks like wedges of watermelon. How could we not try this at home? A layer of lime sherbet is pressed against the bottom and sides of a 2-quart bowl, to stand in for the green rind. Next comes a very thin layer of vanilla ice cream, to simulate the white part of the melon rind. Strawberry sherbet studded with mini chocolate chips stands in for the pink fruit with seeds. This truly is one of our favorite cooking projects, and the result never fails to delight Rose and her friends (and my friends, too). Serve it sometime after a summer barbecue of hamburgers and hot dogs to end the meal with a smile.

1 quart lime sherbet, slightly softened
1 cup vanilla ice cream
1 quart strawberry sherbet
½ cup semisweet mini chocolate chips

1. Line a 2-quart bowl with plastic wrap so it overhangs the side of the bowl by at least 1 inch.

2. Let the lime sherbet soften for 5 minutes on the counter. Spoon the sherbet into the bowl, pressing it into the bottom and up the side with the back of a spoon to form a smooth layer. Place in the freezer for 20 minutes to firm up.

3. Let the vanilla ice cream soften for 5 minutes on the counter. Use a small offset spatula to smooth it over the lime sherbet in a thin layer. Place in the freezer for another 20 minutes to firm up.

4. Let the strawberry sherbet soften for 5 minutes on the counter. Spoon it into a large bowl and mix in the chocolate chips. Spoon this into the bowl containing the lime sherbet and vanilla ice cream so it fills the remaining space and comes to the top of the bowl. Smooth the top and cover with plastic wrap. Freeze for at least 6 hours or up to 1 week.

5. To unmold, remove the plastic from the top of the bowl. Gently tug at the overhanging plastic lining the bowl to loosen the ice cream. Place a serving platter over the bowl, invert, and shake to release. Peel away the plastic, cut into wedges, and serve immediately.

Orange Polka Dot Ice Cream Terrine with Blackberry Sauce *Serves 8 to 10*

This dessert was inspired by my desperate need for a fun, visually impressive, do-ahead dessert made from four supermarket ingredients! I wondered whether I could get a polka-dot effect by layering vanilla ice cream with small scoops of sorbet in a loaf pan and, amazingly, it worked. I like orange, but you may use any contrasting color that you want. Whirling some blackberry jam with a little lemon juice in the food processor gave me a quick sauce. I finally put to use the squeeze bottle I bought at the 5&10 after watching a famous TV chef decorate his plates that way, squirting my sauce over the plates before topping with slices of the terrine. Simply spooning the sauce onto the plates and topping it with the terrine slices will do very nicely, too. The ice cream should be very soft when putting this together, just short of melting. If it starts to get too soft, return it to the freezer for 10 minutes, then continue with the recipe. But make sure that the sorbet is quite hard by keeping the container in the freezer while you spread the ice cream into the pan, so the polka dots keep their shape.

1 pint orange sorbet

1 quart vanilla ice cream

One 12-ounce jar blackberry preserves

2 teaspoons fresh lemon juice

1. Line a 9½ x 4 x 3-inch loaf pan with plastic wrap, making sure the wrap is tucked into all the corners and there is at least 1 inch overhanging the top on all sides.

2. Use a small ice cream scoop to scoop up round balls of sorbet. Place 7 scoops in the bottom of the pan, 4 in one row and 3 in another, so the balls in the rows are not facing each other, but diagonal to each other (this is so when you cut into the terrine every piece will have some polka dots). Place in the freezer until the sorbet is very firm, about 15 minutes. When you put the pan in the freezer, take out the ice cream to soften.

3. Spread a layer of the soft ice cream across the bottom of the pan so it just covers the sorbet, making sure to fill in all the gaps with ice cream. Put the remaining ice cream back in the freezer, then smooth the top of the terrine with a small offset spatula. Scoop 7 more sorbet balls on top of the vanilla layer, as before. Return to the freezer for another 15 minutes to firm up. Take the ice cream out of the freezer before it really starts to firm up.

4. Spread another layer of ice cream on top of the second layer of sorbet balls, filling in and smoothing as before. Cover with plastic wrap and freeze until very firm, at least 6 hours and up to 1 week.

5. Combine the preserves and lemon juice in a food processor and process until smooth. (This sauce will keep in an airtight container in the refrigerator for up to 1 week. Bring to room temperature before using.)

6. To serve, spoon or squirt some blackberry sauce onto each of 8 to 10 dessert plates. Gently tug the plastic wrap that lines the pan to loosen the terrine. Place a large cutting board on top of the pan and turn it over. Gently tap to release. Peel the plastic from the terrine and slice with a sharp knife. Place a slice on each plate over the sauce. Serve immediately.

Stars and Stripes Ice Cream Terrine *Serves 8 to 10*

This simple but gorgeous ice cream dessert is a perfect way to end a barbecue celebrating the Fourth, especially because fresh blueberries will just be coming into season in many parts of the country.

3 pints vanilla ice cream, 2 pints of it slightly softened
1 pint fresh blueberries, picked over for stems
½ teaspoon grated lemon zest
1 pint raspberry sorbet, slightly softened

1. Line a 9½ x 4 x 3-inch loaf pan with plastic wrap, making sure it is tucked into all the corners and there is at least 1 inch overhanging the top on all sides.

2. Combine one of the softened pints of ice cream, the blueberries, and the lemon zest in a food processor and process until smooth.

3. Spread the other softened pint of vanilla ice cream in an even layer across the bottom of the prepared pan. Spread half the blueberry ice cream mixture on top. Place the pan in the freezer until the blueberry layer is firm, at least 1 hour. Place the remaining blueberry ice cream in a bowl and freeze until ready to use.

4. When ready to continue, let the remaining pint of vanilla ice cream and the blueberry ice cream mixture soften for 5 minutes, then spread the vanilla over the firmed-up blueberry ice cream in the pan. Spread the remaining blueberry ice cream on top of the vanilla. Cover with plastic wrap and freeze for at least 6 hours and up to 1 week.

5. Meanwhile, let the raspberry sorbet soften for 5 minutes, then spread in an even, 1-inch-thick layer across the bottom of a rimmed baking sheet. Cover with plastic wrap and freeze until firm, about 1 hour. Use a small star-shaped cookie cutter to cut the sorbet into stars. Using a metal spatula, transfer the stars to an aluminum foil–lined baking sheet. Cover with plastic wrap and freeze until firm, at least 3 hours and up to 1 week.

6. To serve, gently tug the plastic that lines the pan to loosen the terrine. Place a large cutting board over the pan and turn it over. Gently tap to release. Peel the plastic from the terrine and cut into 1-inch-thick slices with a sharp knife. Place a slice on each of 8 to 10 plates and arrange 2 or 3 sorbet stars alongside it. Serve immediately.

Mocha Almond Fudge Sundae Terrine *Serves 8 to 10*

When I was a kid, I used to love to go to Baskin-Robbins with my grandfather. Even though there were dozens of flavors to choose from, I ordered the same one, Jamoca Almond Fudge, every single time I visited the shop. You can still get this old favorite (which has been in rotation since 1959) at Baskin-Robbins shops. I created this nostalgic dessert in homage to the classic.

Nougatine

¾ cup granulated sugar

¼ cup water

½ cup whole almonds, finely chopped

Fudge Sauce

¼ cup granulated sugar

2 tablespoons unsweetened cocoa powder

¾ cup heavy cream

½ cup light corn syrup

2 ounces bittersweet chocolate, coarsely chopped

2 tablespoons unsalted butter

1 teaspoon vanilla extract

¼ teaspoon salt

Terrine

2 pints coffee ice cream

1 pint chocolate ice cream

Topping

½ cup heavy cream, chilled

¼ cup confectioners' sugar

½ teaspoon almond or vanilla extract

1. To make the nougatine, line an 8-inch square baking pan with aluminum foil. Bring the granulated sugar and water to a boil in a small heavy saucepan and let boil, without stirring, until it turns a light amber color, 5 to 7 minutes. If part of the syrup is turning darker than the rest, gently tilt the pan to even out the cooking. As soon as the syrup is a uniformly amber color, stir in the almonds, then pour the rest onto the foil-lined pan, spreading it slightly. Let cool completely.

2. Peel the nougatine from the foil. Coarsely chop into 16 to 20 shards. Reserve half of them for garnish. Place the remaining shards in a food processor and process until finely chopped. (This will keep at room temperature for up to 1 week.)

3. To make the sauce, whisk together the granulated sugar, cocoa, heavy cream, and corn syrup in a medium-size heavy saucepan. Add the chocolate and bring to a boil, whisking constantly. Reduce the heat to medium-low and gently boil, without stirring, for 5 minutes. Remove from the heat and stir in the butter, vanilla, and salt. Let cool to room temperature. (This will keep refrigerated for up to 2 weeks. Reheat until just spreadable, but not hot, before using.)

4. To make the terrine, line a 9½ x 4 x 3-inch loaf pan with plastic wrap, making sure it is tucked into all the corners and there is at least 1 inch overhanging the top on all sides.

5. Let 1 pint of the coffee ice cream soften for 5 minutes on the counter. Spread it in an even layer across the bottom of the pan. Smooth

half the fudge sauce over the ice cream. Sprinkle with half the ground nougatine. Freeze until firm, about 30 minutes. (If the ice cream has gotten very soft, freeze it for 15 minutes to firm up before spreading the fudge sauce.)

6. Let the chocolate ice cream soften for 5 minutes on the counter. Spread over the terrine. Smooth the remaining fudge sauce over the ice cream. Sprinkle with the remaining ground nougatine. Freeze until firm, about 30 minutes.

7. Let the remaining pint of coffee ice cream soften for 5 minutes on the counter. Spread in an even layer over the terrine. Cover with plastic wrap and freeze until very firm, at least 6 hours and up to 1 week.

8. To make the topping, one hour before serving, in a medium-size bowl and using an electric mixer, beat together the heavy cream, confectioners' sugar, and almond extract until it holds stiff peaks. Gently tug the plastic that lines the pan to loosen the terrine. Place a serving platter on top of the pan and turn it over. Gently tap to release. Peel the plastic from the terrine. Spread the whipped cream evenly over the top and sides of the terrine, or place the cream in a pastry bag and pipe it decoratively. Return the platter to the freezer to allow the cream to firm up.

9. Arrange the reserved nougatine shards decoratively on top of the terrine. Slice and serve immediately.

CHAPTER 9

No-Bake Cookies and Confections

This chapter contains a refrigerator full of sweet bites for snacking and gift giving. It's a bit of a grab bag. There are granola bars and fruitcake, chocolate-dipped strawberries and chocolate truffles. Although the recipes may seem to go off in very different directions, they do share something—ease of preparation. Of course, nothing has to be baked. To eliminate further hassle, I've banned candy thermometers and other specialty candy-making equipment. And in the spirit of fun, I occasionally turn to supermarket staples not ordinarily associated with fine desserts: Rice Krispies, graham crackers, and Marshmallow Fluff.

Cookies and bars that are baked puff up in the oven. Cookies and bars that are just stirred together and then refrigerated need something else to give them shape. Puffed rice cereal does this trick for Almond Crisp Candies and No-Bake Granola Bars, the first two recipes in this chapter. Two additional cookie bar recipes use whole graham crackers to give them shape. For both Chocolate Caramel Nut Squares and Chocolate Peanut Squares, a baking pan is lined with graham crackers, and then a gooey caramel and nut mixture is poured on top. The candy topping remains a little chewy, even after being refrigerated. The graham crackers on the bottom give you something to hold on to while you eat.

For Icebox Fruitcake, there is no need to add filler. Fruitcake should be dense and rich, not light and fluffy. The recipe here is beautiful in its purity. Dates, figs, prunes, and nuts are mixed together with some coconut and rum, pressed into a pan, and allowed to come together into a deliciously sticky and dark cake. As with traditional, baked fruitcake, Icebox Fruitcake will keep for a good long time in the refrigerator. Unlike traditional, baked fruitcake, Icebox Fruitcake tastes good enough that it will be eaten before it has to be thrown away or is re-gifted.

The balance of the chapter contains a range of chocolate candies for all occasions. Chocolate is by far my favorite ingredient for making icebox confections. Because it can change from solid to liquid and back again, it is able to take on many shapes and perform many functions. I pour it over dried fruit and nuts to make Tropical Fruit and Nut Chocolate Bites or use it as a dip for strawberries. I combine it with heavy cream and roll it into little balls to make Quick Chocolate Truffles. I cover little disks of sweetened, mint-flavored cream cheese to make Homemade Peppermint Patties.

There is simply no end to the things I want to do with chocolate. But end I must, so I leave you with three recipes for fudge, all of which are based on my memory of the simple fudge I used to make as a kid. It has been many years since I first experimented with the formula, but after all this time I'm still amazed by the magic that occurs when a block of melted chocolate is mixed together with a jar of Marshmallow Fluff and refrigerated for a couple of hours.

Almond Crisp Candies *Makes 36 candies*

Here's a take on a classic back-of-the-box recipe. Instead of using peanut butter, I buy almond butter at a natural foods store. The resulting rounds are surprisingly sophisticated, considering they are made with breakfast cereal! Hazelnut butter and chopped skinned hazelnuts, or cashew butter and chopped unsalted cashews may be substituted. In either case, leave out the almond extract and add ½ teaspoon of vanilla.

½ cup almond butter
1 tablespoon unsalted butter, softened
½ teaspoon almond extract
½ cup confectioners' sugar
1½ cups crispy rice cereal
½ cup finely chopped almonds

1. Using an electric mixer, beat together the almond butter, butter, and almond extract in a medium-size bowl until smooth. With the mixer on low, add the confectioners' sugar until well combined. Stir in the rice cereal.

2. Transfer the mixture to a sheet of waxed paper or piece of plastic wrap, place another sheet on top, and roll into a 12-inch-long log. Press the chopped almonds all over the surface of the log. Cover with plastic wrap and chill until firm, at least 3 hours.

3. Cut the log into ½-inch-thick slices and store in the refrigerator in a plastic container, separating the layers with sheets of aluminum foil or waxed paper. This will keep in the refrigerator for up to 1 week.

 ## Web Guide to Desserts Made with Cereal

I'm almost embarrassed to admit how many hours I've whiled away searching for dessert recipes on Web sites devoted to such products as Rice Krispies and Grape-Nuts cereals. To save you time, here are my favorites, with icebox recipe highlights:

- **www.kelloggs.com.** This is the place to go to find recipes using Kellogg's brand cereals. There are more ideas about how to vary the basic recipe for Rice Krispies Treats than you have ever dreamed of. I urge you to try Kellogg's Crunchy Ice Cream Balls, despite the uninspired name: Combine 3 tablespoons of unsalted butter and 3 tablespoons of light brown sugar in a medium-size saucepan over medium heat and cook, stirring, until the butter is melted and the brown sugar is dissolved. Remove from the heat and stir in 2 cups of Kellogg's Honey Smacks Cereal and ½ cup of chopped walnuts. Roll ½-cup balls of vanilla ice cream in the mixture to coat completely. Place the covered ice cream balls on a parchment-lined baking sheet and freeze until firm, at least 1 hour and up to 6 hours. Serve with caramel sauce or hot fudge sauce, if desired.

No-Bake Granola Bars *Makes 16 squares*

The inclusion of oats makes these bars a wholesome relative of Rice Krispies Treats. I like to toast the oats and nuts in a 350°F oven for 8 to 10 minutes to bring out their flavor. That step is optional, however, so I feel I can still call these treats "no-bake."

¼ cup honey

¼ cup firmly packed light brown sugar

¼ cup (½ stick) unsalted butter

¼ teaspoon ground cinnamon

Pinch of salt

½ teaspoon vanilla extract

1 cup dried cherries, cranberries, blueberries, or raisins

½ cup chopped walnuts

1½ cups crispy rice cereal

1 cup old-fashioned rolled oats (not quick-cooking)

1. Line an 8-inch square baking pan with heavy-duty aluminum foil, making sure it is tucked into all the corners and there is at least 1 inch overhanging the top on all sides.

2. Combine the honey, brown sugar, butter, cinnamon, and salt in a medium-size heavy saucepan. Cook over medium heat until the butter is melted and the brown sugar is dissolved. Bring to a boil and cook, stirring constantly, for 1 minute.

3. Remove from the heat and stir in the vanilla, dried fruit, nuts, rice cereal, and oats. Scrape into the prepared pan and smooth with a rubber spatula. Refrigerate until firm, at least 1 hour.

4. Grasping the overhanging foil on either side of the pan, lift out the granola bars and place on a cutting board. Cut into 16 squares. Serve immediately or store in an airtight container in the refrigerator for up to 1 week.

- **www.kraftfoods.com.** Here you'll find 42 recipes using Post Grape-Nuts, 31 recipes using Post Spoon Size Shredded Wheat Cereal, and 12 recipes using Post Raisin Bran! The standout icebox recipe is Chocolate-Covered Cherries and Peanuts. To make, combine 1 cup of Post Spoon Size Shredded Wheat Cereal, ¼ cup of dry-roasted peanuts, and ¼ cup of dried cherries in a medium-size bowl. Stir in ¼ cup of melted semisweet chocolate chips. Spoon tablespoonfuls of the mixture onto a parchment-lined baking sheet. Refrigerate until set.

- **www.quakeroatmeal.com.** Search "bars" and "cookies" for some surprising and appealing no-bake options. One of my favorites is 3-Minute No-Bake Cookies. To make, combine 2 cups of sugar, ½ cup (1 stick) of unsalted butter, ½ cup of milk, and ⅓ cup of unsweetened cocoa powder in a medium-size saucepan and bring to a boil over medium-high heat, stirring frequently. Boil for 3 minutes. Remove from the heat and stir in 3 cups of Old Fashioned Quaker Oats. Drop tablespoonfuls onto a parchment-lined baking sheet and refrigerate until firm.

Chocolate Caramel Nut Squares *Makes 16 squares*

These are little bites of cookie, caramel, chocolate, and nuts, and they are so much better than a store-bought candy bar!

3½ whole graham crackers, broken into quarters
6 tablespoons (¾ stick) unsalted butter
¼ cup firmly packed light brown sugar
½ teaspoon vanilla extract
Pinch of salt
1 cup semisweet chocolate chips
¾ cup coarsely chopped walnuts

1. Line an 8-inch square baking pan with heavy-duty aluminum foil, making sure it is tucked into all the corners and there is at least 1 inch overhanging the top on all sides.

2. Arrange the graham crackers in the bottom of the pan so they cover it in a single layer (you will have to break up some of the crackers to get a perfect fit).

3. Melt the butter in a small heavy saucepan over medium heat. Whisk in the brown sugar until smooth. Bring to a boil and let boil for 2 minutes, watching carefully and removing if it starts to get too dark. Remove from the heat and whisk in the vanilla and salt. Pour evenly over the graham crackers. Quickly sprinkle on the chocolate chips in an even layer. Let stand for 1 minute, then smooth the melted chips with a small offset spatula. Sprinkle with the chopped nuts, pressing them lightly into the chocolate and caramel. Let cool for 30 minutes, then put in the freezer until the chocolate is firm, about 30 minutes.

4. Grasping the overhanging foil on either side of the pan, lift out the mixture and place on a cutting board. Cut into 16 squares. They will keep in the refrigerator, stored in an airtight container in layers separated by waxed paper, for up to 3 days.

Chocolate Peanut Squares *Makes 16 squares*

Here's a variation on the previous recipe, in which peanut butter replaces the butter, and salted peanuts contrast beautifully with the sugar. The raisins add some chewy texture, but they are optional. These squares are simple but outrageously good.

3½ whole graham crackers, broken into
    quarters
½ cup raisins (optional)
¼ cup creamy peanut butter
¼ cup firmly packed light brown sugar
¼ cup dark corn syrup
½ teaspoon vanilla extract
1 cup semisweet chocolate chips
½ cup coarsely chopped salted peanuts

1. Line an 8-inch square baking pan with heavy-duty aluminum foil, making sure it is tucked into all the corners and there is at least 1 inch overhanging the top on all sides.

2. Arrange the graham crackers in the bottom of the pan so they cover it in a single layer (you will have to break up some of the crackers to get a perfect fit). Sprinkle the raisins over the graham crackers, if using.

3. Combine the peanut butter, brown sugar, and corn syrup in a small heavy saucepan over medium heat and whisk until smooth. Bring to a boil and let boil for 3 minutes. Remove from the heat and whisk in the vanilla. Pour evenly over the graham crackers, spreading with an offset spatula so that it covers them. Quickly sprinkle on the chocolate chips in an even layer. Let stand for 1 minute, then smooth the melted chips with a small offset spatula. Sprinkle with the chopped nuts, pressing them lightly into the chocolate. Let cool for 30 minutes, then put in the freezer until the chocolate is firm, about 30 minutes.

4. Grasping the overhanging foil on either side of the pan, lift out the mixture and place on a cutting board. Cut into 16 squares. They will keep in the refrigerator, stored in an airtight container in layers separated by waxed paper, for up to 3 days.

Tropical Fruit and Nut Chocolate Bites *Makes 36 pieces*

Chunks of dried pineapple, dried mango, and macadamia nuts stirred into melted chocolate make a quick and delicious candy that will keep in the refrigerator for 2 weeks. I chose pineapple and mango for their sweetness and chewy texture, but other dried fruit and nut combinations may be substituted according to taste.

1 pound bittersweet chocolate, finely chopped
⅔ cup coarsely chopped dried pineapple
(about 3½ ounces)
⅔ cup coarsely chopped dried mango
(about 3½ ounces)
1 cup unsalted macadamia nuts, coarsely
chopped

1. Line an 8-inch square baking pan with heavy-duty aluminum foil, making sure it is tucked into all the corners and there is at least 1 inch overhanging the top on all sides.

2. In a medium-size saucepan, bring 2 inches of water to a bare simmer. Place the chocolate in a stainless-steel bowl big enough to rest on top of the saucepan and set it over the pan, making sure it doesn't touch the water. Heat, whisking occasionally, until completely melted. Remove from the heat and whisk until smooth. Stir in the pineapple, mango, and nuts. Scrape into the prepared pan. Smooth with a small offset spatula into an even layer. Refrigerate until firm, about 1 hour.

3. Grasping the overhanging foil on either side of the pan, lift out the mixture and place on a cutting board. Cut into rough chunks with a heavy chef's knife. This will keep in the refrigerator, in an airtight container in layers separated by waxed paper, for up to 2 weeks.

Icebox Fruitcake *Makes 16 squares*

No candied green and red cherries for me—I like a more natural-looking fruitcake, made with rich, dark, dried fruit such as figs, prunes, and dates. Be sure to press the fruitcake mixture tightly into the pan and to weight it down, so it will hold together without baking.

1¾ cups pitted dates (about 8 ounces), finely chopped

1½ cups dried figs (about 8 ounces), stems removed and finely chopped

1¼ cups pitted prunes (about 8 ounces)

2 cups pecans

2½ cups sweetened flaked coconut

¼ cup dark rum

½ teaspoon vanilla extract

¼ teaspoon ground cinnamon

Pinch of salt

1. Line an 8-inch square baking pan with heavy-duty aluminum foil, making sure it is tucked into all the corners and there is at least 1 inch overhanging the top on all sides.

2. Combine the dates, figs, prunes, and pecans in a large bowl. Add the coconut, rum, vanilla, cinnamon, and salt to the bowl and stir well to combine.

3. Transfer the mixture to the prepared pan and press firmly into an even layer. Place plastic wrap directly on top of the fruitcake. Set another 8-inch square baking pan weighted with heavy crockery on top of the plastic. Refrigerate, covered and weighted, for 5 days.

4. Remove the weighted baking pan and plastic. Grasping the overhanging foil on either side of the pan, lift out the fruitcake. Cover tightly in plastic wrap and refrigerate for up to 3 months before cutting into 16 squares.

 ## Other Things to Dip in Chocolate

Although strawberries are traditional, other fruits are equally delicious when dipped in chocolate. The important thing to remember is that the surface of the fruit must be very dry to allow the chocolate coating to set up. For that reason, juicy slices of peach or chunks of fresh pineapple aren't recommended. Seedless grapes and ripe but intact fresh figs will work fine. In addition, all sorts of dried fruits are perfect for dipping: dried pineapple rings, dried mango, dried apricots, and prunes can be transformed into fantastic candy when dipped in chocolate. Refrigerate all fruit, fresh and dried, after dipping. Fresh fruits dipped in chocolate are best eaten the day they are dipped. Dried fruits will keep in the refrigerator, in an airtight container, for several days.

Chocolate-Dipped Strawberries *Makes 16 to 20 strawberries*

The icebox is integral to the success of this recipe. The berries must be well chilled when dipped into the chocolate, so that the chocolate will set up quickly without streaking. The dipped berries must then immediately be refrigerated until serving. Instead of washing the strawberries in water, wipe them clean with paper towels. The smallest droplets of water on the berries will cause the chocolate to seize up. Chocolate-dipped strawberries should be served the same day they are dipped—if you keep them longer than that, the fruit may begin to break down. For special occasions and holidays, you may "double-dip" the berries, first in chocolate, then in sprinkles or small nonpareils in the color of your choice—pink and white for Valentine's Day, green for St. Patrick's Day, pastels for Easter. This makes the berries especially appealing to children. Immediately roll the chocolate-covered portion of the berry in a small bowl of nonpareils before placing it on the baking sheet.

½ pound best-quality bittersweet, milk, or white chocolate, coarsely chopped
2 pints large stem-on strawberries, wiped clean with paper towels and chilled

1. Line a large baking sheet with parchment paper.
2. In a medium-size saucepan, bring 2 inches of water to a bare simmer. Place the chocolate in a stainless-steel bowl big enough to rest on top of the saucepan and set it over the pan, making sure it doesn't touch the water. Heat, whisking occasionally, until most of the chocolate is melted. Remove from the heat and whisk until smooth.
3. Hold a berry by its stem and dip three-fourths of it into the melted chocolate. Let the excess drip back into the bowl, then place the dipped berry on the prepared baking sheet. Repeat with the remaining strawberries, working quickly. Place the baking sheet immediately into the refrigerator and chill until the chocolate is firm, about 1 hour, or up to 8 hours.

Quick Chocolate Truffles *Makes about 40 truffles*

Chocolate truffles are among the simplest candies to make, as long as they are coated with cocoa powder, chopped nuts, or coconut instead of tempered chocolate. By varying the flavorings and coatings, you can create many combinations with this one recipe. If you'd like to make truffles with white chocolate, decrease the heavy cream to ½ cup and increase the butter to ¼ cup (½ stick). Paper candy cups can be purchased at cookware shops and at many supermarkets.

1 pound bittersweet, semisweet, or milk chocolate, finely chopped

1 cup heavy cream

2 tablespoons unsalted butter

¼ cup liquor or liqueur, such as brandy, framboise, Kahlúa, or Grand Marnier (optional)

¼ cup unsweetened cocoa powder, finely chopped nuts, or sweetened flaked coconut

1. Place the chocolate in a large heatproof bowl.

2. Place the cream and butter in a small heavy saucepan and bring just to a boil. Pour over the chocolate and whisk until smooth. Stir in the liquor, if desired. Refrigerate until thick, 2 to 3 hours.

3. Place the cocoa, chopped nuts, or coconut in a small bowl. One at a time, measure out the truffle mixture in rounded teaspoonfuls. With your palms, quickly roll each into a ball and place in the bowl with the cocoa powder, nuts, or coconut, turning to coat. Place the coated truffle in a small paper candy cup. Place them in an airtight plastic container in the refrigerator until ready to serve, up to 3 days. Let stand at room temperature for 30 minutes before serving.

Homemade Peppermint Patties *Makes about 4 dozen*

This is another venerable back-of-the-box recipe, adapted to suit upscale tastes. Instead of chocolate chips and vegetable shortening, I use bittersweet chocolate to cover the creamy centers. Freezing the centers will help the chocolate harden without streaking. Garnished with tiny fresh mint leaves, these make elegant but simple after-dinner treats.

One 8-ounce package cream cheese, softened
¼ teaspoon peppermint extract
One 16-ounce box confectioners' sugar
1 pound bittersweet chocolate

1. Using an electric mixer, beat together the cream cheese and peppermint extract in a large bowl until smooth. Add the confectioners' sugar in ½-cup increments, beating well after each addition. Cover with plastic wrap and refrigerate until firm, about 2 hours.

2. Line a baking sheet with parchment or waxed paper. Place teaspoonfuls of the cream cheese mixture onto the parchment (for perfectly round patties, use a small ice cream scoop). Cover with plastic wrap and freeze until firm, at least 3 hours and up to 1 week.

3. In a medium-size saucepan, bring 2 inches of water to a bare simmer. Place the chocolate in a stainless-steel bowl big enough to rest on top of the saucepan and set it over the pan, making sure it doesn't touch the water. Heat, whisking occasionally, until most of the chocolate is melted. Remove from the heat and whisk until completely smooth. Set aside to cool slightly.

4. Flatten each cream cheese ball into a ¼-inch-thick disk with the palm of your hand. Use a fork to lift each disk and place it into the melted chocolate. Flip it over in the bowl to coat completely. Slide the tines of the fork under the chocolate-covered disk and lift from the bowl, letting the excess chocolate drip back into the bowl. Place each disk on the prepared baking sheet.

5. When all the disks have been dipped, place the baking sheet in the refrigerator until the chocolate has hardened, at least 1 hour. They will keep in the refrigerator, separated by layers of waxed paper in an airtight container, for up to 1 week.

Butterscotch Fudge *Makes 16 squares, about 2 pounds*

Fudge made with brown sugar has a terrific butterscotch flavor, and a wonderful smoothness comes from the cocoa butter in the white chocolate.

1 cup firmly packed light brown sugar

One 7.5-ounce jar Marshmallow Fluff

⅔ cup evaporated milk

6 tablespoons (¾ stick) unsalted butter

½ teaspoon salt

14 ounces best quality white chocolate, finely chopped

2½ cups walnuts, coarsely chopped

1 teaspoon vanilla extract

1. Line an 8-inch square baking pan with heavy-duty aluminum foil, making sure it is tucked into all the corners and there is at least 1 inch overhanging the top on all sides.

2. Combine the brown sugar, Marshmallow Fluff, evaporated milk, butter, and salt in a medium-size heavy saucepan and cook over medium heat, stirring frequently, until it comes to a boil, then let boil for 5 minutes, stirring constantly.

3. Remove from the heat and stir in the chocolate until smooth. Stir in the walnuts and vanilla, then scrape into the prepared pan and smooth with a rubber spatula. Refrigerate until firm, about 2 hours.

4. Grasping the overhanging foil on either side of the pan, lift out the fudge and place on a cutting board. Cut into small squares. Serve immediately or store in the refrigerator, in an airtight container between layers of waxed paper, for up to 1 week.

Chocolate-Cherry Fudge *Makes 16 squares, about 2 pounds*

I must have been about 10 years old when I first made fudge with Marshmallow Fluff. This secret ingredient eliminates the need for the tricky heating and cooling steps used to make traditional fudge. My recipe, adjusted for more grown-up tastes, uses less sugar, more chocolate, and cherry preserves for a Black Forest flavor. It's grown-up fudge, but so easy to make that even a kid could do it.

¾ cup sugar

½ cup cherry preserves

One 7.5-ounce jar Marshmallow Fluff

⅔ cup evaporated milk

6 tablespoons (¾ stick) unsalted butter

½ teaspoon salt

10 ounces bittersweet chocolate, finely chopped

2 ounces unsweetened chocolate, finely chopped

2 cups almonds, coarsely chopped

¾ cup dried sweet cherries

1 teaspoon vanilla extract

1. Line an 8-inch square baking pan with heavy-duty aluminum foil, making sure it is tucked into all the corners and there is at least 1 inch overhanging the top on all sides.

2. Combine the sugar, cherry preserves, Marshmallow Fluff, evaporated milk, butter, and salt in a medium-size heavy saucepan and cook over medium heat, stirring frequently, until it comes to a boil, then let boil for 5 minutes, stirring constantly.

3. Remove from the heat and stir in both chocolates until smooth. Stir in the almonds, cherries, and vanilla, then scrape into the prepared pan and smooth with a rubber spatula. Refrigerate until firm, about 2 hours.

4. Grasping the overhanging foil on either side of the pan, lift out the fudge and place on a cutting board. Cut into small squares. Serve immediately or store in the refrigerator, in an airtight container between layers of waxed paper, for up to 1 week.

Mocha-Almond Fudge   *Makes 16 squares, about 2 pounds*

The addition of espresso powder, cinnamon, and almonds to my basic fudge recipe yields this terrific confection.

1 cup sugar

One 7.5-ounce jar Marshmallow Fluff

⅔ cup evaporated milk

6 tablespoons (¾ stick) unsalted butter

1 tablespoon instant espresso powder

¼ teaspoon ground cinnamon

¼ teaspoon salt

14 ounces bittersweet chocolate, finely chopped

2½ cups almonds, coarsely chopped

1 teaspoon vanilla extract

1. Line an 8-inch square baking pan with heavy-duty aluminum foil, making sure it is tucked into all the corners and there is at least 1 inch overhanging the top on all sides.

2. Combine the sugar, Marshmallow Fluff, evaporated milk, butter, espresso powder, cinnamon, and salt in a medium-size heavy sauce-pan and cook over medium heat, stirring frequently, until it comes to a boil, then let boil for 5 minutes, stirring constantly.

3. Remove from the heat and stir in the chocolate until smooth. Stir in the almonds and vanilla, then scrape into the prepared pan and smooth with a rubber spatula. Refrigerate until firm, about 2 hours.

4. Grasping the overhanging foil on either side of the pan, lift out the fudge and place on a cutting board. Cut into small squares. Serve immediately or store in the refrigerator, in an airtight container between layers of waxed paper, for up to 1 week.

Measurement Equivalents

Please note that all conversions are approximate.

Liquid Conversions	
U.S.	**Metric**
1 tsp	5 ml
1 tbs	15 ml
2 tbs	30 ml
3 tbs	45 ml
¼ cup	60 ml
⅓ cup	75 ml
⅓ cup + 1 tbs	90 ml
⅓ cup + 2 tbs	100 ml
½ cup	120 ml
⅔ cup	150 ml
¾ cup	180 ml
¾ cup + 2 tbs	200 ml
1 cup	240 ml
1 cup + 2 tbs	275 ml
1¼ cups	300 ml
1⅓ cups	325 ml
1½ cups	350 ml
1⅔ cups	375 ml
1¾ cups	400 ml
1¾ cups + 2 tbs	450 ml
2 cups (1 pint)	475 ml
2½ cups	600 ml
3 cups	720 ml
4 cups (1 quart)	945 ml
(1,000 ml is 1 liter)	

Weight Conversions	
US/UK	**Metric**
½ oz	14 g
1 oz	28 g
1½ oz	43 g
2 oz	57 g
2½ oz	71 g
3 oz	85 g
3½ oz	100 g
4 oz	113 g
5 oz	142 g
6 oz	170 g
7 oz	200 g
8 oz	227 g
9 oz	255 g
10 oz	284 g
11 oz	312 g
12 oz	340 g
13 oz	368 g
14 oz	400 g
15 oz	425 g
1 lb	454 g

Oven Temperatures		
°F	**Gas Mark**	**°C**
250	½	120
275	1	140
300	2	150
325	3	165
350	4	180
375	5	190
400	6	200
425	7	220
450	8	230
475	9	240
500	10	260
550	Broil	290

Index